D0198291

Marketing with
Social Media

Marketing with Social Media

10 Easy Steps to Success for Business

Linda Coles

WILEY

First published in 2015 by John Wiley & Sons Australia Ltd
42 McDougall St, Milton Qld 4064

Office also in Melbourne

Typeset in 11.3/14pt ITC Berkeley Oldstyle Std

First edition published under the title *Learn Marketing with Social Media in 7 Days* in 2011

© Blue Banana 20 Ltd 2015

The moral rights of the author have been asserted

National Library of Australia Cataloguing-in-Publication data:

Author:	Coles, Linda, author.
Title:	Marketing with Social Media: 10 easy steps to success for business / Linda Coles.
ISBN:	9780730315124 (pbk)
	9780730315131 (ebook)
Notes:	Includes index.
Subjects:	Social media.
	Internet marketing.
Dewey Number:	658.872

All rights reserved. Except as permitted under the *Australian Copyright Act 1968* (for example, a fair dealing for the purposes of study, research, criticism or review), no part of this book may be reproduced, stored in a retrieval system, communicated or transmitted in any form or by any means without prior written permission. All inquiries should be made to the publisher at the address above.

Cover design and illustration by Wiley

Printed in Singapore by C.O.S. Printers Pte Ltd

10 9 8 7 6 5 4 3

Disclaimer

The material in this publication is of the nature of general comment only, and does not represent professional advice. It is not intended to provide specific guidance for particular circumstances and it should not be relied on as the basis for any decision to take action or not take action on any matter which it covers. Readers should obtain professional advice where appropriate, before making any such decision. To the maximum extent permitted by law, the author and publisher disclaim all responsibility and liability to any person, arising directly or indirectly from any person taking or not taking action based on the information in this publication.

Get a wriggle on!

This book is dedicated to the nicest man in the world, Paul, who happens to be my best friend too. The threat of no birthday present or card if I didn't get a wriggle on was the push I needed to get the original book finished. It just shows what you can achieve if you suddenly become accountable to someone! Thank you, my friend.

Contents

About the author

Who am I?

Hello! I'm Linda Coles, an international speaker and author with short spiky hair.

I run a small company called Blue Banana and mainly work from my home office in New Zealand. Paul is the love of my life, Stella and Monkey are my two cats and Daisy is my goat.

My background is mainly in retail management working for some of the UK's biggest retailers, but life in the slower lane beckoned and so Paul and I moved to pastures green south of Auckland. The slower life never really happened, and I continue to work with some really great brands helping them to build relationships with their customers online.

I speak a great deal and write about building relationships, an important part of being successful in business, and I wrote the books *Learn Marketing with Social Media in 7 Days* in 2011 and *Start with Hello* in 2013. I also write regularly as one of only 500 LinkedIn Influencers, along with Richard Branson, Barack Obama and Arianna Huffington, which sounds very grand and I am very honoured to have been asked.

I hated English lessons at school, and never became interested in writing until about five years ago, when I started blogging and working with social media. I wrote my first book to share my knowledge with thousands of others in order to make it simpler for them to understand. Had I known at my very first job of delivering milk early on weekend mornings I would become a writer, I would have paid more attention at school. Now, I write content for others, so they can pretend they are writing to their client bases, when really it's me.

The team at Wiley is affectionately known in my house as 'Team Wiley', simply a pleasure to work with, and again, people who stretch my mind like an elastic band, sometimes to popping point! The whole editing process is my favourite part, our final chance to make the book as good as it possibly can be, otherwise there is no point in writing it.

Connect with me on:

- ▶ Twitter: @bluebanana20
- ▶ Facebook: www.facebook.com/bluebanana20
- ▶ LinkedIn: www.linkedin.com/in/bluebanana20
- ▶ YouTube: www.youtube.com/bluebanana20
- ▶ Website: www.lindacoles.com, www.bluebanana20.com
- ▶ Google+: https://plus.google.com/+LindaColes
- ▶ Pinterest: www.pinterest.com/lindacoles

Acknowledgements

Writing a book is great fun and hard work and so I would like to give thanks to all of those people who contributed their stories and opinions to this book.

I am continually inspired by the writing of the other LinkedIn Influencers to give informative content as well as to make people think about how they can do a great job with the tools at hand. Once you realise how simple something is, the fear goes, and I know that if you are feeling as if social media is another language, you will be pleasantly surprised. Enjoy.

Introduction

It's not what you know,

It's not who you know,

It's who knows you…

Anonymous

Social media might have some scary connotations for you, but it really need not be like that. If you act online as you do in the flesh, and don't try to be something you are not, it's really very easy.

Who should read this book?

Marketing with social media is something that all brands, both big and small, should now be adding into their marketing mix to make sure they are communicating in the same places that their prospects and customers are hanging out. You may think that marketing with social media does not concern you, but you would be wrong. If your customers expect you to use the relevant sites and you don't have a presence there, they may just look elsewhere, at your competition.

In this book, we will be working through Facebook, LinkedIn, Twitter, YouTube, Google+, Pinterest, Instagram and Vine.

One of the most common questions I am asked is, 'How long is this going to take me?' My answer to that is simple: when you have your LinkedIn, Twitter and Facebook pages all up and running, you have a plan and you have read this book, you need to spend around 30 minutes per day when you first start out. That's just 30 minutes per day on marketing your business and communicating with your prospects and clients.

What will I learn?

By the end of 10 chapters not only will you have a greater understanding of Facebook, LinkedIn, Twitter, YouTube and the others, but you will know more about getting your website to work for you, how to behave online and how to promote your efforts. You will also have created a simple social media plan and a content plan to keep you on track. Also in the book, you will find heaps of easy-to-understand 'how to's' as well as stories about how other companies both large and small are using social media and getting results.

Once you have read the book and completed the activities, you will be well on your way to creating your very own successful social media presence.

Enjoy! Then make it happen.

Opening story

On a very wet and rainy Friday morning in June, one of those torrential downpour types of days, the traffic on the motorway was at a standstill: we were going nowhere. I had been on the motorway for nearly two hours on what should have been a 60-minute journey, and it was obvious I was going to be late for my appointment.

I made the call to my first appointment and postponed it for another day, then got off the motorway. As I now had a little time to spare before my next appointment, I grabbed a coffee and picked up a *Business Today* magazine from the bookshop. On the front cover was the country manager for Microsoft New Zealand, Kevin Ackhurst, and I knew I had to act. I had had an idea a couple of weeks previously, but had not done anything about it; now there he was looking at me from the magazine rack — it was an omen, surely.

I wondered if he was on LinkedIn and could I contact him through there?

Of course he was — most businesspeople are. And to my delight, I discovered he was in one of the groups I was in, which meant I could send him a message directly without knowing his email address.

I wrote a quick note to him with my idea, and sent it off. To my surprise, he responded within a couple of hours to say he liked my idea and was passing my details on to the team and they would be in touch.

True to their word, they did get in touch to organise a meeting. Woohoo! I'm talking to Microsoft!

Do you think that if I had simply picked up the telephone, fought my way past the gatekeeper, introduced myself and hopefully managed to explain my idea to such a senior person, I would have gotten that far?

I don't think so.

By using LinkedIn to my advantage, I cleared any obstacles right out of the way and went straight to the person I needed. I made it easy for him to find out more about me simply by clicking on my name, and from there he could decide if I was worth seeing or not.

This is a simple use of a great business-networking site that has the ability to connect businesspeople with other businesspeople, all across the world.

CHAPTER 1
What is social media? Policy, plan and profitability

Key areas we will cover in chapter 1:

✓ social media explained

✓ growing your business with social media

✓ making an effective social media plan

✓ what makes people share?

If you think **social media** is a fad for the young ones and that you are too old to even contemplate it, never mind finding the time or having the resources to do it, then you should read on.

What is social media and is it a fad?

I have heard people say, 'I have no time for social media', to which I respond, 'You have no time for marketing your business and building relationships with prospects and customers?'

Think about that for a moment.

Yes it takes effort, but so does every aspect of running a successful business, and there are tools available to help you pull it all together. When we put our plan together later on in the chapter, you will see how easy it will be.

You may also think that your customers and prospects are not on social media, and so social media can't help your business. Did you know that the fastest growing demographic on **Facebook** is females over 55, or that **LinkedIn**'s most popular sector is 'service', with personal profiles for everyone from cheese-makers to the President of the United States? There will be a group of people, however large or small, on these channels just waiting for you to put yourself or your brand on their radar.

How cool would it be to get your customers' feedback in real time, as it is happening? You'll get both good and not-so-good comments, but the not-so-good comments are as valuable to your business as the good. If the comments show you have an issue in your business that needs fixing, it's better that you know about it, isn't it? You can then apologise, react to the issue and make it good, for everyone to see.

Social media is way past the 'it's a fad' stage, and is definitely at the 'getting results' stage.

Sharing your life and finding new friends online is the norm for the younger generation. But while I don't want to share my private life with the masses, I am okay about sharing my business life with anyone who is willing to listen.

Your details are not safe online. Or are they?

The more nervous among us are concerned that all of our details are out there for anyone to steal. But your details can be secured on the vast majority of social media sites, and controlled by yourself (although you do need to double-check your settings occasionally as sites make updates). Remember, too, that your business details — your mobile phone number, your landline and email address — are likely already available for all to see on your website, because you want it to be easy for a prospective client or customer to get in touch with you. Of course I wouldn't suggest you post your address if you work from home, or other sensitive information, but my point is the choice is yours as to how much to share, and you want your business details out there, so it's a bit of a non-issue.

How are you marketing at the moment?

What do you have in your current **marketing toolkit**? I suspect it contains things like newsletters, your website, news media articles, internal communications, surveys, TV and radio, events, referrals and the good old telephone business directory. Most if not all of these tools will have a price tag attached to them, with some being out of a lot of companies' reach. It is not every company that can afford to advertise on TV, and certainly not enough to be effective with an advert over time. Not only can these tools be cost-prohibitive, they can also be a little out of date.

Now consider the social media and online sites that are becoming more and more commonplace. You might not even class some of them as social media, but they are online communication channels nonetheless.

The beauty of social media from a cost point of view is that there really doesn't need to be any costs involved, apart from your time, so if you are still hanging on to your business directory ad as the most secure way of generating new enquiries, it could be time to think again and move on to something new.

Table 1.1 lists some of the current and new marketing tools.

Table 1.1: current and new marketing tools

Current marketing tools	New marketing tools
Newsletters	LinkedIn
News media	Twitter
Website	Facebook
TV and radio	YouTube
Business directory	Blog
Referrals	Webinars
Surveys	Forums
Intranet	Podcasts
	Other social sites

Table 1.2 gives some examples of how to use the new marketing tools in place of the old.

Table 1.2: uses of new marketing tools

New marketing tool	Use	Current marketing tool
YouTube	Record seminars Demonstrate products Engage your customers	In-person demonstration Newsletters Telephone
Facebook	Build new relationships Engage with your customers Increase brand exposure	Networking events Telephone Newsletters Static website
LinkedIn	Networking business-to-business Build your business connection base Promote useful articles online	Networking events Online personal website Newspaper and magazine articles
Twitter	Publish your articles Short conversation posts	Newspaper and magazines Telephone

So what exactly is social media?

The term 'social media' can be broken down as 'social', because you are being social, and 'media', because it is published on the web. It is simply a platform for a conversation that is online rather than the more conventional ways in which we communicate, and so it gives us access to many people at once; the internet has given it scale. You can look at it in two ways: brand awareness, which can be a personal or a business brand; and **networking**, or building relationships online. The two do cross over, because as you are networking, your brand is becoming more visible at the same time.

I separate the two because I think they can be two quite distinct activities, and through this book I will be sharing with you different stories about how people and companies have used social media in both ways to get their desired result.

From a branding point of view, social media platforms enable you to engage with your customers in real time and find out what they want, think or feel at any given time, which makes them a great tool for any company to utilise.

Benefits of using social media

There are many benefits to using social media:

- It's free.

- You have a huge audience.

- It's another communication tool to be utilised alongside more traditional methods.

- You can engage easily with your customers.

- You will have a visible presence on the web.

- You receive real-time feedback.

What choices of social media sites do I have?

The obvious choices of social media sites are Facebook, LinkedIn, **Twitter** and **YouTube**, with others starting to make waves all the time such as **Google+**. To these we can add online channels such as blogging, **webinars**, **Skype** and **podcasts**.

Long gone are the days of picking up a pen and writing a letter to someone, putting a stamp on the envelope, and walking to the postbox to send it—it just doesn't really happen anymore. Email is now the normal form of business communication, with the telephone a close second, but as more and more people are in email overload, I can see that changing. You just can't get through your emails and do your work in the allotted time, and who wants to do it when they should be spending time with their family or asleep? The way we communicate has changed, and will change again in the future.

Using social media sites such as Facebook, you can keep in touch with friends or colleagues by leaving a quick message on their wall rather than sending an email, or by sending a tweet if it is only a short message. To make it easy to connect with others, people now have their social media details, rather than their fax number, on their business cards. Who uses a fax anymore?

Table 1.3 summarises the main social networking sites.

Table 1.3: social networking sites and their uses

Site	Web address	Use
LinkedIn	www.linkedin.com	Business-to-business networking
Facebook	www.facebook.com	Social and business-to-customer site
Twitter	www.twitter.com	Small bite-size messages to all
YouTube	www.youtube.com	Video-broadcasting site
Google+	www.plus.google.com	Business-to-business and business-to-customer

So I'm networking at the same time?

Social media is an extra way of talking to your customers and clients in different **forums** where they are hanging out. It is also a way of networking online, so rather than being tied to an event date and time, networking online is open 24/7: you can do it in your pyjamas in the morning with your cornflakes, or do it in your pyjamas in the evening with a glass of wine, whichever suits your time and business needs. This is particularly helpful if your prospects or clients are in another time zone. It does have a social element to it or else why call it social media, but I prefer to call it networking online, unless of course I am on Facebook for pleasure on my private page, chatting to my close friends and family.

You could also look at the people that are following you or your fans as a tribe, or a focus group on steroids. Once you have a tribe of followers, be it online or not, put them to work. Ask them what they need or desire and see if you can provide it.

What if it goes wrong?

As I mentioned earlier, social media sites enable you to receive real-time feedback, both positive and negative. Recently the NYPD came under fire when they decided to engage with the local community via Twitter. The NYPD set up and promoted the hashtag #myNYPD—it was meant to encourage people to share great photos they might have of themselves with the police in the community. Instead, some decided to use it to post pictures the police would rather you didn't see, such as individuals being dragged by their feet as they were removed from protests. As long as you act quickly when things don't go according to plan, you can minimise any damage.

How will social media grow my business?

Some companies have been able to grow their business massively because of how they have cleverly used this marketing tool.

But how can you do it? Simple. You need to:

▶ engage your customers

▶ listen to your customers

▶ build your **business network**

▶ find your **cheerleaders**

▶ do it all over and over again.

Engage your customers

You may be wondering just what I mean by this, but it is simple. Get your customers interested in what you have to offer. What problem do they need fixing, what need do they want to fulfil, what desires do they have that are not being met? This is your chance to engage them with a solution, a solution just for them.

Listen to your customers

By talking and listening to your customers and prospects, you will get a feel for what it is they really want from your product or service. Now you are not likely to sit and call each and every one of your customers, you may not even have their details to be able to do so, but by using the social media sites where they hang out, you have an easy set of tools at your disposal to be able to listen effectively.

Build your business network

Building your business network of connections will give you tentacles in all sorts of different industries and places: you may never know how and when you will use them, but they are there for you. By building a large connection base, you can call on select people to point you in the right direction, or reach out to them for help with a quirky need. I am only two degrees away from the President of the United States on LinkedIn, so if I am ever in Washington, maybe I will look him up ... But seriously, a connection recently reached out for help with a quirky position he had, and I passed his request on to one of my connections, and guess what, it was a fit. It doesn't always work out quite that easily, but I know that without a great connection base, I wouldn't have the same resources to make use of from time to time.

Find your cheerleaders

You will have customers and clients who absolutely love what it is you do — they couldn't be happier with your product or service. So how are you currently leveraging from them and rewarding them? Do you even know who they are?

If someone has been a cheerleader of yours without you realising it, do something special for them. Make them cheer some more, and maybe they will shout about you and your brand more than they already do, including online where they hang out.

Do it all over and over again

'Giapo' is an ice-cream parlour on Auckland's Queen Street near the Civic Theatre. Set up in January 2009 at a time when business was definitely getting tougher, Gianpaolo Grazioli took the plunge and it seems he hasn't looked back. Not only is the shop set up in a very funky and modern way, but he has also made a huge splash and gained large numbers of followers and fans with the way he has used social media sites such as Twitter, Facebook and YouTube. There is always something going on in his shop, whether it be karaoke, ice-cream tasting or even organised runs around the CBD. The message is relayed back and forth through the online social media space for massive exposure. You can even shoot a quick video while still in his store and upload it to YouTube for your mates to see. Talk about getting others to promote your brand for you and become cheerleaders! He also encourages customers to bring in fruit from their gardens that have not been sprayed with any nasty chemicals, and he will pay you in 'Giapo dollars' or ice cream. It's a great way to engage your customers both on- and offline, and a real example of how a small operator can create a buzz about their brand.

Let's start networking and making connections

By using sites such as LinkedIn, you can network effectively and make use of other people's connections that you may want to do business with.

I recently asked a question in a group on LinkedIn and a lady from Canada responded. She said she could help me, but knew someone a bit closer to home to me — could she pass my details on? I agreed, and a couple of days later I received a phone call from Sarah. She said my name was familiar to her and asked if I was attending a women's networking luncheon later that day, which I was. You can imagine, then, that when we both arrived at the function, we made a beeline for each other. It was almost like seeing an old friend again because we had been joined together by the lady in Canada, and we had this great story to tell others. Sarah later became a client and a good friend, and in fact lives only 40 minutes down the road from me, so don't be put off if you think networking online is for talking to people from other countries and is of no use to you. The world is an incredibly small place now with the use of technology, and doing business even across the other side of the world may not be that hard.

Networking in your pyjamas

If I said to you that there was a networking event taking place nearby and some of the greatest businesspeople you would like to know will be attending, would you make the effort to get to the event? Of course you would, but that is going on all the time on social networking sites such as LinkedIn. Couple that with the ease of Twitter, and you have a recipe for nurturing relationships with people you may not ordinarily come into contact with.

There would not be many people who would read the Yellow Pages or another business directory with a view to calling and meeting new business connections, so apart from regular networking events and business appointments, how else can you grow your business network? Face-to-face networking options such as your local Chamber of Commerce and other business networks will never die — they are undoubtedly the best way to meet other business connections — but online networking can and will simply run alongside as an alternative and extra way to meet people, and it will give you the variety you may be lacking. You are not constrained by a venue or time; you can take part at any time of the day that suits you or your business.

Benefits of networking online

The benefits of networking online include the following:

- You can do it 24/7, 365 days a year, at a time to suit you or your business needs.
- It's not location-specific.
- It's a less pressured environment.
- You can do it in your pyjamas.

Create a listening post

What about listening? Social media can also be used as a simple **listening post**, enabling you to hear what is being said about a multitude of things, whether it is your brand, your own name or even your competitors. There are tools to enable this to happen easily, so you don't need to regularly search through Google to hear what others may be saying about you.

Listening online gives you the following benefits:

- ▶ You can respond to bloggers who have mentioned your brand or your name.
- ▶ You can promote positive mentions.
- ▶ You can deal with any negative mentions.
- ▶ You can monitor your competition.

Tools for listening include:

- ▶ **Tweetdeck**—a dashboard tool to make Twitter easier to use
- ▶ **Google Alerts**—set up an alert for a given keyword to your inbox
- ▶ **Twitter search**—search Twitter for **keywords**; no account needed
- ▶ Radion6 (not free)—a corporate tool for listening on the web.

Get an effective social media plan together

If you don't spend a little time making a **social media plan**, you will more than likely end up attacking it from all angles and your success may be limited, which will only make you feel like the whole thing was a waste of time. If you really hate writing plans, you don't need to worry too much because your plan really only needs to be a simple one-pager. You just need some clear direction so that you know where you are headed and can track your successes. As Jack Welch once said, 'A strategic plan is simply picking a general direction and implementing it like hell.' So true, and my kind of guy.

How do I go about making my one-page plan?

First you need to ask yourself what you want to achieve from using social media in three, six and 12 months. It could be:

▶ a larger prospect base to talk to

▶ a certain number of connections and followers

▶ a monetary amount

▶ a reputation for being an expert in your field

▶ a certain number of visitors to your website.

Then ask yourself three questions:

▶ What is my *purpose* in using social media?

▶ What am I hoping to *achieve*?

▶ What is my desired *outcome*?

The 'purpose' aspect could be very simple, such as:

▶ You don't want your competitors gaining the edge because they are already using social media.

▶ You realise it is another way of communicating with your prospects.

▶ You want to grow your business network of connections.

The 'achieve' aspect could be:

▶ You want to attract more customers.

▶ You want to listen to what is being said.

▶ You want to gain more brand exposure.

The 'outcome' aspect could be:

▶ You have created and engaged a tribe of fans who have become cheerleaders for your business.

▶ You have a listening post set up.

▶ You have a greater network of business connections.

You set the figure for the goal.

A template for making a social media plan is provided in table 1.4 (overleaf). See appendix A for a sample completed social media plan. Social media moves and changes so fast that it would be difficult to plan much further ahead than 12 months, but it is important that you have the milestones along the way at three and six months, just to check how you are tracking against your goals and to see if you need to make any adjustments. You may also find that your goals have changed slightly, so this also needs to be taken into account.

Activity 1

Complete your social media plan.

Table 1.4: social media plan

What is the purpose?	What are our 12-month social media objectives?
What will it achieve?	What are our six-month social media objectives?
What is the outcome?	What are our three-month social media objectives?
Our target market is:	Measured by:
	Team:

Create a SWOT analysis

Another element to consider adding to your plan is the good old-fashioned **SWOT analysis** (strengths, weaknesses, opportunities, threats), which, although it has been around a long time, is still a very effective and easy-to-use tool.

By making a list of the four headings, and asking the questions of your business, you will end up with four clear areas that will show where you may have problems and whether you are travelling in the right direction. Take into account what your competition is currently doing, or what you think they might do. Copy the template in table 1.5 or download it from my website www.lindacoles.com/resources. See appendix A for a sample completed SWOT analysis.

Table 1.5: SWOT analysis

Strengths	Weaknesses
Opportunities	Threats

The SWOT analysis can be done as part of your plan, or as an activity on its own. Either way, it is important to see, from a social media point of view, where you and your competitors are currently.

▶ *Strengths.* What are you good at? List your strengths and then see how you can leverage them for even greater results.

▶ *Weaknesses.* What are you not so good at? What do you need to do to mitigate your weaknesses?

▶ *Opportunities.* What are the events and trends that are favourable to you? How can you leverage your opportunities?

▶ *Threats.* What are the events and trends that are not favourable to you? How can you mitigate your threats?

Activity 2

Complete your SWOT analysis.

Who is my target market?

Follow the SWOT analysis by asking three more questions about who you want to communicate with:

▶ Who is your **target market**?

▶ What are the characteristics of the market?

▶ What is their biggest problem, need or desire?

If you know your business well enough, these should be easy enough to answer.

Beware here: what you think is your target market may in fact not be at all, so I suggest you take a look at the characteristics of your current clients and jot down some notes. Which ones on the client list:

▶ pay your invoices on time

▶ are no bother for your team to deal with

▶ buy from you repeatedly (if applicable)

▶ give you referrals

▶ love your product or service

▶ have the potential for growth?

With those characteristics in mind, what do they all have in common to become your target market? Is it turnover, location, industry or something else? But are they your most profitable clients?

Have a quick look at the clients who:

▶ pay your invoices late

▶ take up too much of your time

▶ squeeze you dry of margin

▶ whine and gripe at your team.

You may not want too many of those clients. In fact, you may want to drop a few of those if you have them! Likewise, if your clients are in a dying market such as video rental stores, there is no potential for growth for them and so your client base may also be diminishing.

Once you have answered these three simple questions, you are ready to move on to the next part of making your plan, and that is deciding who will run your campaign and where the resources will come from.

Forming the social media team

A common mistake is for a company to see who has a bit of bandwidth, or who is under less pressure than the rest of the team, and is therefore presumed to have the time to set up your social media sites. That can very often be the receptionist. Now although your receptionist may be fantastic at his job, he may not necessarily be a marketer or customer service manager, so who should be working on your social media sites?

I asked a couple of companies how they decided who should be on the **social media team**. One company said, 'The people need to be online already and understand how it all works, they need to be on brand, so they live and breathe our business, and lastly they need to be on resource. The latter refers to a good knowledge about where they can find great content in our market that is useful to share out again.'

Another company said, 'We simply sent an invitation out to the whole company to see who wanted to be involved in the first place, who are our knowledgeable team players that know and understand our business and the online space? From there, we made our selection.'

Both of these ideas are great ways to find the correct person or persons for your social media plan, but if you are a very small company, it may just be you in the first place. Don't despair that you are already trying to balance more plates in the air than you would care to admit; if you stick to your plan, you won't go far wrong and your efforts will be rewarded.

Get a media team in place

Don't feel that you have to do it all yourself, and certainly don't simply get the most junior team member to do it as she spends so much time on Facebook. Ask your staff who would like to be involved, create a small team and call them the 'media team'. If you don't have such a team, consider who else from outside your business might want to be involved. As long as you or a designated person has the final say, knows exactly what is going on and is accountable, you should be fine.

Get a content plan

Content, or what information you choose to share from around the web or your own work, is what will make your efforts succeed: no-one wants to read uninteresting articles. Brainstorm with your colleagues and anyone else you wish to get involved, and make a list of the useful websites that always have great content on your chosen topic. You can add those sites to your **content plan** template later. Those sites may not even be local to you but on the other side of the world—that doesn't matter. If you have a bridal business and your chosen resource sites are in New York, who cares? You are adding value back to your followers, fans and connections with your expertise and knowledge about what is happening on a larger scale, or, in the case of fashion, what trends are developing.

When you have found the best resource sites, subscribe to their databases so that the best and most interesting articles come straight to your inbox for you to read and action. That way you don't need to revisit their sites each day to see if there is anything new.

Keep a list of the resources you are going to be using so that regardless of who is looking after your social media, anyone in the team can update it should the need arise. It also means you just don't have too much to think about each day, as you know where your content is coming from.

Don't make it all links back to other people's sites; you want to balance it out with great information from your own team including photos, video clips and stories.

Set up content themes

Depending on what your business is, you might want to theme your content to match your overall marketing plan. This is easy if you are, for example, a florist or gift shop: make a list of all of the events that happen throughout the year and theme your content accordingly.

On Valentine's Day, the florist could have not only matching flowers, but also short articles on the history of St Valentine's, as well as images. A great discussion topic for LinkedIn could be 'What are you doing for your partner this Valentine's' — a question designed to get others networking and nothing else.

For a health professional, it may be 'spine awareness week', so focus on that. Ask questions on LinkedIn about posture and how people deal with back pain.

If you are a mechanic, you might want to talk about the importance of good brakes during the winter months on your Facebook page and Twitter.

There are other areas that are on the content plan such as:

▶ off-topic questions

▶ useful videos

▶ article ideas.

As you read through the book, these areas will be covered in the various sections, so fill these in as you go.

You can copy the template content plan in table 1.6 or download it from my website www.lindacoles.com/resources. See appendix A for a sample completed content plan.

Quick ideas for your content

These are just a few ideas to get you thinking in the right direction; they are covered in more detail later in this book.

Facebook

News topics could include:

▶ what has been happening in your industry

▶ team announcements

▶ funny stories

▶ your company **blog**.

You could also upload videos of your products or services, and some photos.

LinkedIn

LinkedIn has a more business feel to it, so your content should mirror this.

▶ Use some of those great links you have found as a discussion point in the groups you are a member of.

▶ Write articles for your own website on a weekly or monthly basis and refer to those.

Table 1.6: content plan

What is your target market's BIGGEST problem, need or desire?	Themes for the quarter
Articles to write	Useful videos
Off-message questions	Useful websites

Twitter

The conversation here is a mixture of formal and informal, a bit like an office party.

▶ Tweet your own articles and blog posts.

▶ Tweet content from the LinkedIn groups if those groups allow it.

▶ Pass on or **retweet** other people's interesting articles.

YouTube

Upload videos that:

▶ showcase your product

▶ introduce the team

▶ show your TV commercial.

What makes people share?

There is a science behind what makes people share and as social media success really does rely on people sharing your content, it's important to create the right type of content. There is a simply great book on the subject called *Contagious: Why Things Catch On* by Jonah Berger, which is also published by Wiley. Berger is a Wharton professor and it's a fabulous read that will totally blow your mind about just what the vital ingredients are. Jonah has given me permission to briefly write about those secret ingredients here but I still suggest you add his book to your reading list. Consider the following, and decide which elements you think make the most sense to your audience and how you can create something worth sharing.

Social currency

People love to share things that make them look good. They like to look smart, funny and in the know. That might be by using gamification (making something game-like) or by being the first to have seen a video or to answer a question. That feeling of a little smugness, I suppose, and we are probably all guilty of it at some time.

Triggers

We talk about things that are top of mind or topical, and so using a reminder that keeps an idea about your brand in people's heads really works. What is it that makes people think about your product or idea? Are you a pizza restaurant and Saturday night reminds people that it's pizza night? Or how about when you have your morning coffee you think about having a KitKat? Saturday and coffee are both triggers in these cases.

Emotion

When we care, we share. Think of all the YouTube videos or images you have shared in the past and look at what it was that made you share them. No doubt there will have been an emotion involved; maybe something made you laugh heartily, made you angry or sad, or feel totally in awe. Whatever it was, it altered your pulse rate, which in turn makes you inevitably pass it on. What can fire people up about your product or service?

Public

Built to show, built to grow. Can others see when someone has consumed your product? For example, if you have an iPhone or iPad and you send emails from them, there will be a default message at the bottom of each one saying 'sent from my iPhone'. This is public advertising and sharing without you even thinking about it, as well as a little bit of showing off that you own a **smartphone**. Each time you send an email, you are doing the advertising for Apple products—how can someone else do the same for you?

Practical value

News you can use. If you come across something really useful or helpful, you will more than likely share it with your friends. It might be advice on unruly teenagers, money-saving tips, healthy-eating recipes or how to make the perfect exploding volcano model. Whatever it is, useful gets shared. What problem does your product or service solve for others? That is what you need to focus your message on, then find a medium to deliver it.

Stories

Stories are easy to remember and pass on. If you can dress your message up in a true story rather than a bunch of facts and figures, it will become more memorable. The trick here is also to find a way to incorporate your brand and make people remember it. Think of great series of ads like the Oxo stock cube lady and her family—those 42 ads ran for 16 years and the family became a part of many British households.

The Countdown grocery chain ran similar ads with a ficticious family called the Colemans, which also ran for many years, keeping the Countdown brand in many homes, both on TV and online.What Trojan horse ideas could you use to get your product known?

Rules of engagement

It is important to set some guidelines as to what can and can't be said on the various sites, and it is up to you how detailed you want the document to be. The guidelines can be simple and include the following:

▶ Never swear.

▶ Never bring the company into disrepute.

▶ Never badmouth the competition.

▶ Never argue with another company.

▶ Deal with all complaints as if the complainants were standing in front of you.

▶ Don't shout in capital letters.

There are plenty of social media policy examples available online and some for purchase, so take a look at what others have done and what you feel is appropriate for your business. While you want to make sure everything is covered, you don't want to go over the top.

Activity 3

Create your content plan.

Monitoring your social media profitability

We have looked at why we are using social media, who we want to talk to and what we want to achieve. We have a list of where the content is going to come from and who is going to manage it. The last thing to work out is how we are going to measure our **return on investment** (ROI).

There has been a lot of discussion about measuring the ROI of your efforts as people realise it is in fact quite difficult to measure, but there are a few tools to look out for.

A great free piece of software is **Google Analytics**. Your social media efforts are going to drive lots of traffic back to your website, so make sure you have monitoring tools installed to capture that information. By monitoring your traffic, you can see which sites are in fact referring traffic back to your website and chart it. From your Google account simply click on 'Analytics' and follow the easy steps. You will then be given a short piece of **HTML code** to put into your website. You may need your web person to do this bit for you, but it only takes a couple of minutes so shouldn't cost much, if anything.

Facebook Insights is another free tool available to you. This will give you information on the mix of your fans and how active they are, which you can then use for marketing purposes. For instance, if the majority of your fans are female aged 35 to 44, and you decide to try **Facebook ads**, you can target those people for a more focused advert.

LinkedIn is maybe a little easier and more obvious, as you know if you connected with someone on LinkedIn and they became a client after a series of meetings. That is hard evidence. It is worth mentioning at this point that not everyone will become a client straight away and some never will, but from a networking point of view, who knows where that connection might take you? When you send a valuable newsletter-style message to all of your connections (see chapter 5), watch what happens to your own inbox with positive comments coming back in to you. Remember that radar?

By registering for a **bitly** account at www.bitly.com you can monitor just how often a tweeted link has been opened, so how many sets of eyeballs have now had exposure to your information, and therefore how successful that piece of information you shared has been to others.

Other areas that contribute to the ROI

Defining the ROI of social media is a bit like defining the ROI of your telephone — it's not easy. But there are more questions to ask that will contribute to your ROI:

▶ What have we learned from our customers that we didn't know before?

▶ Did we manage to talk to more prospects and expose our brand even more?

▶ Did our clients find out anything new about us?

▶ Are our staff more engaged now?

▶ What shall we do for all of our cheerleaders?

How great would it be if you found out on your Facebook page that the new cheese-flavoured crackers you have just spent a fortune developing were in fact a little over-salted for most people's taste, and you were wondering why repeat sales were not happening as much as you would like? What a goldmine of information you could have at your fingertips.

Why not reward your cheerleaders and get them to cheer about your product or service even more? Send them some free product for even more promotion.

What you don't see

During a recent conversation with a company director, he told me about a prospect that had called him after doing his due diligence on his company. If he was going to part with a large amount of money, he wanted to see if the company practised what it preached. He looked at the team's LinkedIn profiles to see if they were all of the same standard and displayed the same company message, checked that the company Facebook page followed suit, and maybe even looked at some of the other sites to see if everything was 'on message'. It wasn't. It wasn't consistent all the way through.

Now if that person had not picked up the phone and called the director to tell him what he'd found, he might have simply decided not to become a client and no-one would be any the wiser. What it did do was make the director's company sit up and take note that it needed to get its message consistent, and pronto. How many other prospects had it lost that they didn't know about because its social media message was not consistent?

People are checking out your brand all over the internet, so if you have anything to tidy up, do it today.

Conclusion of chapter 1

Now you understand a little more about what social media is and how it can help your business. The most important thing to do next is create that plan, because without it, your efforts could be seriously diluted and your success is at risk. We will refer back to your plan as we work through the book, so before you move on to the next chapter, do spend some time, perhaps with your team, and get at least the bones of it together. As this plan is a working document, keep it handy for the relevant people to work with and update.

CHAPTER 2
Facebook basics and content ideas

Key areas we will cover in chapter 2:

✓ choosing which page to use for business or pleasure

✓ content ideas for a successful page

✓ Facebook ads and what they should include

✓ managing your fans.

Facebook was originally set up for people who wanted to keep in touch while at college and university, but the site has morphed into something much more than that. With over one billion users registered, and about 70 per cent of those users living outside the US, it is a global phenomenon.

Quick stats www.facebook.com

Here are some interesting Facebook stats:

▶ there are over one billion users worldwide

▶ 50 per cent of active users log on daily

▶ the average user has 130 friends on Facebook

▶ the fastest growing demographic is females over 55.

Using Facebook for marketing

As marketers see the growth and the possibilities of this site, more and more brands are setting up **business pages** and seeing some real results from interacting with their customers. By getting real-time feedback, both good and bad, from their business pages, marketers can now really interact and engage with their customers, and for free too.

So where do you start? There are many page types to choose from. Which one is for you?

Personal page

The **personal page** is simply for individuals to keep in touch with their friends on a social level, and not for business. You will occasionally see people using it as a business page but there are a few things to note about doing so:

▶ It is against Facebook's terms and conditions, so you risk being closed down.

▶ You have to be a member of Facebook to join in.

▶ You have to become a friend of that person to join in the conversation.

▶ Profile pages are not easily seen by Google, depending on the individual's security settings.

▶ You can have a maximum of 5000 friends.

Community page

Community pages should be avoided. They can be automatically generated by any given topic, but can't be edited or updated, making them a bit of a nuisance. Steer clear for now.

Group page

A **group page** is an option if you are running a club or cause. The group can be open to anyone to join, closed so it's invitation-only, or completely private, such as for a small company's **intranet** system.

Points to consider about a group:

▶ You can send an email to all members that they see in their inbox.

▶ Like-minded people can discuss things in relative privacy.

▶ You need to be a member of Facebook to join in.

▶ Group pages are not easily seen by Google, depending on if the group is open or closed.

Business page

The most practical option for most businesses, the business page is easily created and you don't need to be a member of Facebook to see it.

Other points about business pages:

▶ Pages are easily seen by Google.

▶ A small business could use a Facebook page as its first website.

▶ Facebook is free to join and use.

▶ One billion people on Facebook could potentially see your page.

▶ Updates feed into your fans' own newsfeed as you post something.

▶ When your fan likes or comments on a post, their friends see your page name in their newsfeed too, so the viral effect gets to work.

A business page is by far the best option for most people, so let's look at how you can set one up.

Setting up your business page

Once you have decided to create a Facebook page for your business, you need to know how to build it.

There are two ways of setting up your own business page on Facebook. The first is the most common way, but you need to have a personal account with Facebook in order to create your business page. To build your page, simply click the 'create page' link from the drop-down menu of your profile page and then follow the easy instructions.

The second way is to go straight to www.facebook.com/pages/create and again follow the simple instructions.

There are pros and cons to everything, and choosing which way to build your page is no exception. There are a couple of main differences for each option:

▶ If you run your business page off a personal profile, you own the page and can access it to update it.

▶ You can and should allocate trusted members of your team as 'admins', which means they will also have access to the business page for updating it. They will not, however, be able to see your personal profile page, only their own, which means they must have their own Facebook account.

▶ Any admin can delete another admin, so choose your team carefully.

▶ By running your page off your profile, you have the ability to share any of the content with your own Facebook friends, and the other admins can share content with their friends.

▶ If you choose to run a business-only account, there is a little less functionality.

▶ If you run a business-only account, you have no friends to share information with.

Once you have decided which way you are going to go, choose which category of page you would like to make. The categories are as follows:

▶ *Local business:* this really is for a bricks-and-mortar store, cafe, restaurant and so on, as the page gives you an area to add your opening hours and bus route. With a places page, people can check in from their smartphones when they physically visit your premises, alerting their friends as to where they are. Great for restaurants and cafes.

▶ *Brand, product or organisation:* this is probably the most common as there is plenty of room on the info tab to write all about what it is that your company does, when it was founded, links to sites and so on.

▶ *Artist, band or public figure:* depending on which sub-category you pick, there are different areas within the info tab. For example, if you pick 'politician', there is plenty of room to fill out set questions such as what party you are running for, further detailed information about yourself, and all of your contact details.

Whichever category you choose, you can switch it later if you need to, perhaps if you see something that is more relevant.

When you have chosen your page and filled in the basic details, take care with the page name as it can only be changed if you have fewer than 100 fans/likes. After that, you are pretty much stuck with it, although you can apply to Facebook and ask them to change it. This is not a given though!

Your page name has now been created but your page is pretty bare and useless.

Activity 1

Choose your page type and create your business page.

Making your page look good

Load up your company logo straight into the small image holder. This could be a picture of you if you are a sole proprietor and you are the business. While it's always great to see the face of who is managing the page, a logo is far more eye-catching in the newsfeed and great for brand exposure.

The hero or large image space is also very important and you can get creative here. Since Facebook created this image space some time ago, they have changed the rules many times about what you can and can't put there, but I think it will always be safe to say create an image that signifies what your business is all about. I change mine regularly because events come and go, books are launched and seasons change, so why not? Make use of this space as you can. Check back with Facebook to the current set of rules, though, so you don't breach any conditions.

Welcome page

A welcome page is simply a default page that new visitors who are not yet fans land on, instead of the usual page. There are many companies that offer apps to help you create extra pages, or you can get your website people to create something for you, but the apps tend to be cheaper. A welcome page allows you to make a good first impression, like a window display. You can again get creative here:

▶ Add a video containing a quick welcome message either about what to expect from becoming a fan or about your company.

▶ Add a humorous video with a 'click the like button' message embedded in your image.

▶ Add your newsletter sign-up form.

▶ Add a reason to join in: why should someone 'like' your page?

Take a look at some examples of what the big brands are doing, such as Coca-Cola, Red Bull and others. While they have bigger budgets than most of us, there is no harm in looking at their ideas and adapting them to fit your business.

You will still need to get someone with some coding experience to do this for you, or you could subscribe to one of the many welcome page apps that are available.

Activity 2

Set up your welcome page with one of the many apps to choose from, such as TabSite.

Applications

There are many **applications** (apps) you can add to your Facebook business page and here I have listed just a few of the most popular ones. The majority of Facebook apps are free, but some do have a small charge, much like your smartphone apps. These apps make in essence another page of information attached to your Facebook page.

▶ TabSite is a very popular welcome page app that will also give you an extra row of pages to play with. There is a free version for a straightforward welcome page or you can upgrade it for adding video and other things. Visit www.tabsite.com.

▶ foursquare is a location-based app that allows you to put a map on your Facebook page to show visitors exactly where you are. You must first register your business with www.foursquare.com/businesses. Again, it works best for cafes, stores and other places people frequently visit. To install it go to www.apps.facebook.com/placewidget.

- **Instagram** will feed your Instagram photos in to another page so your fans can see an extra bunch of images from your brand. You can do the same with your **Pinterest** feed and YouTube feed, so lots of your brands' social presence can be accessed in the one place.

Activity 3

Review and choose which apps you want to add in.

What sort of content should you put on your Facebook page?

There are two types of content for your page — on topic and off topic. On topic is everything to do with your page's topic, no matter how broad, and so could include industry links and articles as well as your own news. Topics can be educational or inspirational.

Off topic is anything random that can be used to generate a little engagement or conversation on your page, to get people talking. I have found that what seem like quite mundane questions have in fact generated the most comments and interaction. I have asked questions such as 'What are you doing this holiday weekend?' or 'Which famous person would you most like to have a coffee with and why?' This simply gets people on your page talking and only takes a few seconds to think about and comment on.

Some simple questions you could ask:

- What is your favourite smartphone app?
- What are some of the best books you have read?
- What is the dumbest thing you have done this week?
- How do you motivate yourself when it's rainy?

Do you need multiple pages?

Some companies have several brands under the main company umbrella and so you may decide to have more than one Facebook page to separate things.

If you are a catering company that specialises in weddings and corporate events, you might want two separate pages. Even though you are one brand, there are two distinct sides to the business, one being bridal catering and the other a more corporate focus for business lunches and events.

The bridal page could include not only bridal catering, but other things bridal such as possible venues and photography. This makes the Facebook page almost like a portal site, where a bride or groom could find out all sorts of information to help create their big day, all in one place.

Other articles and blog posts you could share on your wedding catering page include:

▶ events from the weekend, including photos

▶ prestigious events you have catered for — name-dropping always helps

▶ wedding photos

▶ wedding cakes

▶ video of an event

▶ edible gift ideas for your guests

▶ timeline of making the great wedding cake — what was involved

▶ food at recent celebrity weddings — what they ate

▶ dealing with dietary requirements for the bridal party

▶ links to the bride and groom's blog about the day if they have one.

In all cases, be sure to add just enough detail about what is happening in each posting. It is no good putting up your lovely pictures of the buffet lunch if you have not gone into loving detail about what was on the buffet. Keep the readers' mouths watering as they read all about the mini pastries oozing with soft, dill-flavoured cream cheese and delicate pieces of gently smoked salmon—you get the picture. You are trying to convince readers to think of you when it comes time for them to place their own order.

You can also think of more personal content, such as what the team has been up to recently, competitions your staff may have been involved in, new team members or even funny stories about what happened during an event. The list is endless.

So what can you do with the corporate catering page? You could add:

▶ venue ideas for your party

▶ ideas about wines to accompany the food

▶ recipes to make at home

▶ reminders to book catering for key dates such as Easter, Valentine's Day, Christmas

▶ food trivia questions and competitions

▶ recommendations from happy customers

▶ links to articles published about the company

▶ new corporate vehicles on the road

▶ food-tasting events

▶ daily dinner recipe.

And on the list goes ... food is such an easy one!

Back to your plan

Your content plan is crucial to your page's success, so spend the time to make it and actually use it.

You don't need to write everything that you post on your wall: you simply don't have the time to keep that up. Find resources on the web that are in line with your brand and that complement each other rather than compete against you. Think about the following:

▶ What websites do you read regularly to keep abreast of your industry?

▶ What sites are there that perhaps do compete in your space, but are overseas and so not a local threat?

▶ What other sites are local to you that you could help promote on your page and build a relationship with for referrals?

▶ What sites complement your page? For example, wedding planners and wedding caterers.

Your content plan will pretty much make or break the success of your page. By not having a plan, you will find it very hard to keep being creative and get the right sort of content for your fans, meaning they may lose interest and go elsewhere.

By brainstorming with your team, you will not only get buy-in from them to ensure your page's success, but many heads are better than one when it comes to thinking up ideas.

It is also a good idea for more than one person to update the page, so that sickness and holidays are covered and the page keeps up its momentum. If there is more than one person updating the page, perhaps sign off your post with your first name so your fans know who they are talking to when they comment, and you know who posted what from the company point of view.

Following are some content ideas for various industries.

▶ *Real estate.* Listing all of your properties that are currently for sale is somewhat boring for your page visitor, who can see that information on the company website in most cases, so there's no need to duplicate it. Interest as many people in your page as you can so that when it comes to be their time to sell, your informative page is still on their radar. All they need to do then is get in touch. When people are looking to purchase a house, they may need extra information such as:

- what to look for in the sale contract
- where to find a good lawyer to handle the transaction
- where to find a good reliable builder if there's some work needing to be done
- garden design
- interior decorating
- bargain properties
- local surroundings — schools, amenities.

▶ *Garage mechanic*. You may wonder what you could possibly put on a mechanic's page to appeal to a greater audience. One possibility would be to target it to females who want to keep their vehicles running smoothly themselves: you will probably have a captive audience if you get your message right. There are not many garages that are focused on helping women specifically. But if you are not a petrol-head, why would you become a fan of a garage page? How about if it had information on:

- how to change a tyre
- what warning signs to look out for, such as green brake fluid leaking
- car reviews
- open days
- learning the trade
- what different parts of the engine do
- wet-weather car care.

▶ *Accountant.* This is another subject that could be brought to life to cover its many different aspects, if done well. Consider information on:

– how to calculate how much money you should be putting away for your tax at the end of the year

– keeping your business plan current

– helping with cash flow

– seminars (invite your fans and clients)

– deciphering technical terms to make them easily understood

– planning for selling your business

– general business advice.

▶ *Retail shop.* Your shop probably has a website, which will pretty much be an online brochure with opening times and contact details, and you may also have a shopping cart to allow you to sell online. So your Facebook page could be a great meeting place for discussion, depending on what you sell. Imagine you own a cycle shop, and your customers love hanging out in your shop to see what is new and discuss their last race and their upcoming events. They can now do it both in your shop and online. Cycling is a lifestyle choice and many riders are very passionate about it, so this gives you the chance to capitalise on that passion even more. With a hobby such as cycling, you tend to have friends who are also heavily into cycling, so your fan page has the opportunity to really make use of the viral effect. Your page could include:

– upcoming events

– cycle maintenance

– race reports

- special offers
- new product discussions
- coaching tips
- flash new cycle images
- race video.

▶ *Vineyard*. Now this would be an interesting page for quite a few people. Include:

- how the grapes are grown
- a video of wine being made
- what makes a good wine
- discussions on what makes a great flavour
- special offers and open days
- corporate tours
- wine reviews.

In all of these examples you should also add interesting company news, photos of products or team members and video footage of products in action or being made if you manufacture something. The more interesting (and sometimes basic) the information, the better: you might know your industry or products well, but your average visitor may not, so use the opportunity to educate at the same time.

Other things to add to your Facebook page could include links to articles on other websites that you think may be of interest, although the danger in doing this is that your visitors may not come back to your own site, so they might not see the rest of what you have to offer. On the other hand, they may come back more frequently because you have a balanced offering of other people's work on the same or a similar topic that is as interesting as your own. Find the balance between what suits your business and what your fans want. You could even try asking them.

When you do post something to share with your audience, always add a call to action. For example, ask a question or make a statement and add on the end 'we would love to hear your comments' or 'click "like" if you agree'. That way, people know you want them to do something, and generally they will if it takes only a second or two.

With all of that in mind, consider what resources you could marry up with to make your page an even greater source of information for your visitors.

Activity 4

Jot down what you could put on your page from what you have learned so far.

Should you allow your fans to post on your page?

Why do some big brands and well-known celebrities not allow you to post on their Facebook wall?

Apart from the annoying activity of others posting spam messages and plugs for their own business or activities, I can't see a real reason — it doesn't seem a fair way of interacting with the fans, and it really defeats the point of the page.

In the name of research while writing this book, I wanted to become a fan of a well-known car manufacturer's page and ask what made the car so special to them, but it wouldn't let me post. I would have thought that car enthusiasts all over the world would want to be able to interact with their favourite brand. Move over to Starbucks, and its page is full of interaction and postings from anybody and everybody about their experiences with Starbucks products from all corners of the world.

I can understand why Barack Obama's page, with well over 40 million fans, has the facility turned off. Can you imagine the mass of postings from real fans and those that just want to take a pop? Managing the comments alone would be a full-time job, with some of the postings from Barack's team running into the tens of thousands of comments as replies. That really is simply not doable.

If your page is purely another online brochure, and you have one because you are expected to have one, you probably want to take the road with the least amount of hassle or work, in which case you would turn the facility off. I would not advocate even having a Facebook page if you are not really going to use it, so think about your reason for doing it before you get started.

If, on the other hand, you really are trying to generate massive brand awareness, network and engage with your customers and build up a loyal tribe of fans and followers, then you will need to have the resources to back it up. If, like Barack Obama, you have the 'problem' of millions of fans, simply let your fans know what to expect in the way of answers. Manage people's expectations by posting a note in the info tab or other visible place on your page that you will be able to reply to only a handful of comments each day. That way, everyone knows where they stand.

A couple of extra things to note about your page:

▶ Determine how much access to your page you want your fans to have. Did you know you can choose whether to allow them to be able to post images and videos to your wall?

▶ Don't overstuff your wall with constant messages all day. One or two posts per day should be enough.

▶ Do post great images of your product or service with a link to further information.

▶ Don't post pictures of the team when they are drunk at their Christmas party.

Spam filters

Facebook has also introduced **spam filters**, but they can sometimes be a little overzealous, so get into the habit of regularly checking what has been filtered from your page. You will find the spam filter in your activity log. From there you can decide what is actually spam and delete it, and repost anything that is not.

Comments

Reply to all comments by using the person's name, just as you would to that person if they were standing in front of you, and be friendly and helpful at all times. If you do happen to get any negative comments, don't simply delete them unless they are particularly abusive or rude. By deleting negative comments and keeping a clean page, you may be adding fuel to a smouldering fire. Others will be watching to see how you react and deal with a negative comment, so do something about it. If you find that your page is getting quite a lot of negative feedback about your product or service, you need to do something about that whole issue within your company, so it's great information to have. You might never have known there was a problem without that feedback. We cover Facebook etiquette in chapter 5, so more about that then.

Scheduling content

There is also an option to schedule your posts, which means that your posts will go live at a time and date specified by you. This is particularly handy if you have a full day ahead or perhaps you are away for a couple of days: your Facebook page will still receive fresh content that you have pre-loaded. Look for the clock icon under the status update box.

Facebook ads

Facebook ads are a great way to get traffic to a particular place as you can really drill down to who you want to talk to.

You can choose who to target by:

▶ *location*—within 50 miles of a town

▶ *demographics*—male, female, age group

▶ *interests*—just about anything!

▶ *connections* on Facebook—users who are connected to certain criteria including certain pages.

Once you have decided to have a go with Facebook ads, you need to consider four things:

▶ What is the goal of the ad?

▶ Who are you trying to reach?

▶ What is your daily/weekly budget?

▶ Who is going to monitor the results?

What is the goal of the ad?

Now you might think this is obvious: you just want more fans, right? Well, not necessarily. It may be that you want more people to visit your website rather than your fan page, as you have a sale on or a new collection being launched. In this case your ad may be pointed straight to your chosen website landing page for visitors to find out more.

If your goal is to generate brand exposure and gain more fans to communicate with, your ad should be pointed to your Facebook page rather than your website.

The advantage of pointing your ad to your Facebook page is that when your visitor clicks 'like' and becomes a fan, you can then communicate with them through their Facebook newsfeed or by sending them an update. By sending your visitors to your website, there generally is no way for them to interact with your site and those visitors may never return, so you have lost them. Relying on them to join your mailing list may be too much to expect.

Who are you trying to reach — what is your target market?

Again you may think this is obvious, but bearing in mind how you can drill down into the Facebook database, you may have a different message for different people. Check out what you concluded in your social media plan for your target market to make sure you are targeting your ads correctly.

Let's say you are a coffee shop and you want to create an ad to drive traffic to your Facebook page to generate more fans. Your customers could be split into three categories depending on age and wants, and so the three different messages could read as follows:

▶ *Mums* — bring your little ones in for a milkshake and get a free chocolate bar when you mention Facebook.

▶ *Students* — take a break from studying and grab a hot steaming mug of creamy latte. Have a free chocolate bar on us when you mention Facebook.

▶ *Older* — we are now open until midnight, so call in for a hot chocolate before bedtime and get a free chocolate bar on us when you mention Facebook.

You get the idea? It's a different message for different age groups, but the same product. You have a maximum of 25 characters for the title, and 133 for the body, so you may need to fiddle around with your message to make it fit.

What is your budget?

You can set it at as much or as little as you want to spend, so if you are a small company and have a budget of only $50 per week, then that is a start. Obviously the more you spend, the more visible your ad will be.

The more targeted your advert is, the smaller the number of people who will see it, but the more relevant it will be to those who do see it. You can actually create an ad that is seen by everyone in your town who is aged 35 to 40 and is a fan of a particular page, maybe even the Facebook page of your competition. Very cool, and very targeted.

Monitor and refine your ad

Someone has to monitor your ad or ads and make adjustments where necessary. In the early days that can take a little time to do while you are getting used to it.

Check your stats daily and watch for any trends. If you're not quite getting the results you had expected you may wish to stop the ad and start another ad that is almost the same, changing just one thing such as the image or the heading. Slight changes can make a world of difference, but only change one thing at a time or you won't know what the successful change was.

Again, monitor your results and test another aspect before doing it again. Once you are really happy with the results and with how much you are spending, you can afford to let it run for a while. Keep monitoring it though, as you may find the ad's effectiveness will dwindle in time and you need to start the process again.

Facebook also has a great self-help area on Facebook ads, so click the 'build audience' link for more information.

Keep in mind that most people are on Facebook for entertainment, they are not there searching for what you have to offer, so your ad needs to stand out both visually as well as the text message in order to get people to click on it.

Sponsored stories

Another type of ad is sponsored stories, which is simply the promotion of a post gone by. Both sponsored stories and regular ads have the option of being seen in the newsfeed or just down the right side of a regular computer screen: you choose when you set them up. When they are shown in the newsfeed they are also visible when viewed by a smartphone, and as about 50 per cent of Facebook users access Facebook via their mobile, that's an important point to remember. Personally I don't use the ads anymore, but I do use sponsored stories.

Facebook is a business too, out to make money, and as they don't charge you to use their site, they have to make their revenue in other ways—ads. As long as you target your ad to the right demographic including age, sex and location, you won't go too far wrong, so as I said at the beginning, make sure you decide on who your target market actually is—it really is important.

Activity 5

Create an ad for your brand following the advice in this chapter.

Social media success story: Budget Car Sales

Budget Car Sales is a secondhand car yard on the outskirts of town and they are doing extremely well generating and converting leads for used-car sales on their Facebook page. It's not always been that way, though: when I started working with them, while they had a decent fan base of around 2000, most of their fans were not even in the same country, and it was obvious the 'fan base' had been bought. Why else would 75 per cent of their 'fans' want to become a fan of a secondhand car yard on the other side of the world? It just didn't seem likely.

The company wanted to change their Facebook page name because their brand had changed, and obviously everything needed to be consistent. The problem was, Facebook declined the name change, so they were stuck: they had to decide whether to stay as they were or start again. It was a tough decision because it's not easy to accumulate fans in the first

(continued)

Social media success story: Budget Car Sales *(cont'd)*

place, and what about all the past content that would then be deleted too?

A new page was created and they posted a 'we are on the move' image on the old page with the URL to the new one. They decided to run two pages alongside each other for a period of a month so that they could let the real original fans know they would be shifting, and so on each post, they also included a link to the new page asking fans to join them there. This worked a treat, allowing the new page to have a good few fans straight away, leaving them thinking about how creative they needed to be to get the numbers back up.

They created a content plan, which included funny vehicle videos from YouTube, wacky car images and related ideas from Pinterest as well as actual vehicles for sale in the yard, car care tips, finance options and happy shopper selfies. Posting daily and scheduling posts for the end of the day, when they knew their fans were online the most, were also key. The content proved to be a success, with a good mixture of funny stuff as well as the serious business of selling cars, and they added in a few giveaway competitions to see what would be popular. They gave away cinema tickets for two asking 'who would you take along with you?' in the hope fans would tag their friends. (It's against Facebook's terms and conditions to stipulate friend tagging as a way to gain more fans.) While it was popular, it wasn't as popular as giving away $100 fuel vouchers! That really made things hot up, so I guess giving away something of value that is also related to the product being sold is the key to finding a giveaway that works—and with the price of fuel, it's a no-brainer.

The yard also runs events at their premises, which would be promoted through Facebook's events app. As the event organiser they can get a rough idea of how many people from Facebook will be attending, and it's great to actually meet some of their virtual customers and say hello in person, which will also surely deepen loyalty.

They also added an email marketing campaign to their database to encourage others to become a fan, and told them what they could expect from the page including giveaways and special events.

The last weekend promotion at the yard was a resounding success with previous records smashed, and while it was not all down to Facebook, without getting the message out there to prospective customers and starting to engage with them, they wouldn't have had the same number of visitors to the yard.

Their fan base has now well overtaken what they had on their old page and their fans want to engage and refer, so they have developed a small gold mine other car yards would love to have access to! If you want to be successful on Facebook, find your target market, decide on your budget and deliver what they want to hear, consistently.

All this happened through hard work from the marketing co-ordinator and a little help from having a small budget for sponsored stories, because you do have to be realistic in getting people to find your page and become a fan on Facebook. How else will they see you?

Conclusion of chapter 2

Facebook is becoming a marketer's dream; the site gets better and better as the months go by. There are so many apps that are available to you to really turn your page into something special, with some great functionality that you probably otherwise would not be able to afford. When you have your content plan in place, you really will need to spend only a few minutes in the morning posting your information, and a few minutes again in the afternoon checking to see if you have any comments that need answering.

CHAPTER 3
LinkedIn basics and networking using LinkedIn

Key areas we will cover in chapter 3:

✓ personal profile content

✓ networking and making connections

✓ making the most of groups

✓ creating your own company page.

LinkedIn's main function is networking with people you would not ordinarily come into contact with. By connecting with other like-minded people, you can effectively build your business connection base, and have the potential to grow your business.

This chapter will work through the real basics that often get missed when people set up their LinkedIn profile, and then move on to how to actually use it to get real results. We will cover what should be in your profile, adding in rich media content to really give a full 3D effect, and networking for success. We will also cover setting up a company page for even more online presence.

Quick stats www.linkedin.com

Here are some interesting LinkedIn stats:

▶ number one business-to-business-only networking site in the world

▶ more than 300 million members worldwide

▶ adults only although starting to allow students

▶ open 24/7 for networking

▶ database of prospective contacts

▶ two new members join every second.

Your personal profile

Don't underestimate how many people will be checking you out online, and LinkedIn is definitely the easiest place to start looking. Whether you are meeting a new prospect for the first time, or have sent a connection request to someone, you can bet your bottom dollar that they will have looked you up or clicked back on your name to read your profile to find out more. Wouldn't you?

The first thing to mention is that your profile has to be your name rather than your company name because it is you we are interested in networking with, not your business. It is also against LinkedIn's terms and conditions to do otherwise.

If you take a look at your own profile page now, would you be happy with how it is representing you or your company, or could it be better? I am guessing it could be a whole lot better.

It is worth investing a little time one rainy Sunday afternoon, when the rest of the family is watching a movie, to getting it right. I would suggest putting a couple of hours aside to do it, but bear in mind it is never finished. It will always be a work in progress that you will add to as time goes on to keep it fresh and up to date.

Your professional headline or title

Most people make the assumption this should simply be their title — for example, director at your company — but that doesn't necessarily tell someone looking at your profile what it is you do. With a company name like Blue Banana, you couldn't possibly know what the company does, unless you have heard of it, so 'Director at Blue Banana' means nothing.

The professional headline area gives you 120 characters including spaces to work with to really create something precise, and filled with keywords if at all possible. It really needs to be the essence of what you do. Mine says 'Speaker, Trainer and Content Creator. Author of *Start with Hello* and *Learn Marketing with Social Media in 7 Days*'. By adding in the titles of my books, I am adding in vital keywords in order to be found and also exposing my authority on the subject by telling everyone I am a published author.

Beware

Make sure you write this piece of text for your prospects, and not the search engines, as a professional headline stuffed with keywords could be detrimental to your own branding. Quite often you will see a person's email address or mobile telephone number in this area, which is against LinkedIn's terms and conditions, so again, beware. You can always add those in further down your page.

Your image

The image that you add of yourself should be a close-up head and shoulders, rather than a picture of you way off in the distance with your fishing rod — save that for Facebook.

When you do eventually meet up for a coffee with someone from LinkedIn, it helps to know what he or she looks like: you don't want to rely on looking for the 'red rose', so to speak. Think also about the professional image your personal brand is portraying:

have a photo that reflects that. Having no image gives me the impression the person doesn't want to be seen and I wonder why. Having a great image also means you are seven times more likely to show up in search results, so give yourself a chance.

The status update box

This box is here for you to post heaps of interesting things as and when they happen. For example, if you are being interviewed for a TV show tonight, have an article appearing in a well-known publication, are running an event, or just simply have some great news to share, this is the box to put it in, and it's on your home page. When you update this box, simply post a teaser sentence about what it is you are sharing and a link to it. The box will automatically populate, then just click 'share'. You can also share other files with your connections such as interesting PDFs and PowerPoint presentations here.

At the time of writing, LinkedIn had just started to roll out a longer post option within this box via the pencil icon, which means you will be able to create longer posts, add video and images to them and share your posts with your connections. Back in 2012 LinkedIn gave the long post option to 150 worldwide Influencers and I was lucky enough to be one of them. Now this option is slowly being rolled out to everyone. From experience, I can tell you it's great to be able to use this as my main blog and have a ready-made audience to interact with. It's a great tool and I strongly recommend that you use it.

You can get a huge amount of great content to share from LinkedIn's Pulse or newsfeed on your home page. This is where some of the best and most shared content on the web is filtered into, depending on what you have opted in to receive, as well as posts from LinkedIn's now 500 Influencers all around the world. These are thought leaders and businesspeople who write on the LinkedIn platform to share their wisdom with the rest of us about business topics mainly, which gives another dimension to the content available.

Some ideas you may want to share:

▶ articles you have written that appear online

▶ introducing new team members

▶ details about an exciting project about to start

▶ a job vacancy

▶ an upcoming TV interview

▶ a link to a useful YouTube video

▶ an upcoming event that you are running or attending.

Activity 1

Add the ideas for your update box into your content plan.

Whatever you post in this box will appear on all of your direct connections' home page activity, so they can see what is going on in your business life. Think of it as a rolling newsletter—so don't post uninteresting or spamming content—and you can also tick the Twitter box to feed that same piece of information out to Twitter at the same time.

You will notice other people's updates in your own newsfeed and under them you have some options to share:

▶ *Like*. Similar to Facebook, you can simply click on anyone's status update's 'like' button to show approval for the posting without feeling you have to leave a comment, and that puts you on their radar for a moment again.

▶ *Comment*. Feel free to leave a comment about a connection's post, as by doing so, you are again putting yourself back on that connection's radar and also publishing the article and comment into your own newsfeed. It's great when people do this with your content because it really helps with the viral spread, leading to many more eyeballs taking in your post.

▶ *Share.* This gives you the ability to share the status update box content with others. You can share your connections' content back to your own box, or share with groups that you are a member of on LinkedIn. You also have the choice of sending it as a tweet either just to your LinkedIn connections that are on Twitter, or to everyone you are connected to on Twitter: it's a very easy way to spread exciting or useful information to others.

Your website details

LinkedIn gives you three hot links: areas that when clicked go through to another site that they have been pointed to. Those three links need to be put to good use.

Often you will see a person's profile making use of only one of the links, because they have only one website. But why not use all three of your links and point them to three different pages on your website, such as your 'services' page, 'about' page and 'special offer' page? You can point them to your business Facebook page, your blog or even a club website that you are a member of. Either way, you may as well make good use of them.

The trick here is in the drop-down box. Select the option 'other'. This then creates a bit of choice. Yes, you can simply choose 'my website' or 'my blog', but by clicking 'other', another box appears for you to type in what the page you are sending visitors to is all about.

Your public profile address

The purpose of this feature is to allow you to **hyperlink** to your LinkedIn public profile address from your email signature or a job application. That way, the person is able to read the correct profile, which is particularly useful if there is someone with the same name as you but with a less salubrious past. To do this, simply click 'edit' next to your public profile address while in edit mode, and set it to your name. Then whenever you want to direct someone from, say, your email signature to your page, you simply have to set up a hyperlink within your email signature that they will be able to click on.

If your name has already been reserved, why don't you try adding in your middle initial or name? If, like me, you don't have a middle name, you could use your social media username (mine is bluebanana20). Sadly, even all those years ago when I started out in social media, the name Blue Banana was already taken.

Your summary

This is another really underutilised part of the profile, which surprises me as it seems like a simple thing to fill in. To do it right, though, takes a bit of thought. You have space for 2000 characters in all, so you have a reasonable area in which to write about yourself. But what should it contain to get the most benefit?

To my mind it should say:

▶ who you are and what you do

▶ what makes you different from your competitors

▶ why someone should use you rather than your competitor

▶ something light-hearted and interesting about yourself such as your sailing ambition or your weekend-warrior activities.

Write this piece of your profile in the first person rather than in the third person, to make it more personal and real. When you have finished, just check down the left margin and see how many times you started a sentence or paragraph with 'I': you may find you need to change a few for another choice of word. This is picky, I know, but plenty of prospects or clients could be reading your summary and they will pick it up.

Additional information and personal information

Put as much or as little in these two areas as you feel like doing. With 'additional information' you can add clubs and associations that you belong to such as Rotary, Entrepreneurs and so on, and add in important achievements you have attained in your life. I rode my bicycle around Lake Taupo, which is 160 km and hard work, let me tell you, so I am proud and pleased with my achievement. I put it on my profile so that others can see I am a keen cyclist, and if I am meeting someone and their profile also mentions they are a keen cyclist, it gives us a point to connect the conversation immediately. I find it a real icebreaker.

The 'personal information' tab is visible only to those who are directly connected to you or whose email addresses are in the system after uploading your contacts but you are not necessarily connected to. I add my contact details but it's a matter of personal preference whether you disclose your marital status or not.

Activity 2

Complete the additional information section. Include some things that interest you such as your sports and hobbies.

Other sections

There are also other sections that include areas for you to add:

▶ certifications

▶ languages

▶ patents

▶ projects

▶ publications

▶ test scores

▶ courses.

I hope LinkedIn works on a way to allow you to sort the order of your current positions if you do more than one thing at a time: the position with the most recent date on it, for example your volunteer work, will automatically load up to the top, which might not be appropriate.

Skills

Adding skills to your profile does more than you might think. Firstly, they are searchable so when someone is searching through LinkedIn for what you do, you come up in the results. Secondly, you can endorse a connection's skill and they can do the same to you. This then populates the visual box with their photo in the skills section and adds another to the count over on the left side. You will see a mini picture of who has endorsed you for what, which is a great visual when someone is looking at your profile and there are many endorsements for your skills. This may give you the edge over the competition. When you receive an endorsement from someone, you will be notified via LinkedIn email so you know who has done it. Turn endorsements around with you endorsing someone else, it puts you back on their radar just for a moment, which is always a good thing.

Rich media

You can also add some great visual content to your profile, which really makes your profile stand out because so many people just don't bother with it. So what can you add?

▶ *PowerPoint* — Add a PowerPoint presentation with a handful of great slides about what it is that you do. Make sure you add a final page with your contact details on it and either post this to your profile directly, or better yet, load it up to a **Slideshare** account (www.slideshare.net). As LinkedIn owns Slideshare, it's another free place that your content can get access to another bunch of viewers. You can then link your Slideshare account to your LinkedIn account, or simply post the link to it on your profile. While in edit mode, use the odd-shaped icon over on the right that looks a little like a square with a plus sign attached to it.

▶ *Video*—Use this same icon to upload a YouTube video to your profile. You can also upload the whole file if you wish.

▶ *PDFs*—PDFs are a great way to add terms and conditions, price lists, brochures and the like so that your connections can download them easily.

▶ *Links*—You can add a link to anything here, such as articles you have written on another site, news stories about your company, the list is endless.

Whatever you add to your profile via the rich media square icon, make sure it's visually appealing to allow connections to see the best from you.

Some LinkedIn profile dos and don'ts

Do:

- write your summary in the first person; that is, from your point of view rather than someone else's

- write your profile content for human readers rather than the search engines

- use the three website links to web pages of your choice

- make sure your grammar and spelling are correct

- add skills to be found easily as well as showcase them.

Don't:

- fill your summary with a sales pitch

- start each sentence with 'I'

- add your email address or telephone number in your professional headline

- use a full-length photo as your image—we can't see you

- use all capital letters (shouting).

> ### Activity 3
>
> Create your LinkedIn profile and get someone to critique it for you.

That covers the basics of your profile, but there are some very cool applications that you can add to really show yourself off in a good way.

Recommendations

This is another overlooked area: I don't think people realise the importance of **recommendations**. The average person on LinkedIn has less than a handful, with many people not having any at all. As a great percentage of us trust word-of-mouth advertising, or recommendations, and not many of us trust advertisements, it makes sense to have recommendations from satisfied clients and customers visible for all to see. They can also stand you in good stead when you are in the market for a new job as they can be used almost as references, and that may be the one thing that sets you apart from the other candidates.

I think a good number to aim for is 10, although there is no harm going for more as I think the more people can endorse your work, the better it is for you. Be true with your recommendations, though. Don't ask your close friends, neighbours and half of the team at your place of work to write one: that simply looks dumb. A recommendation simply saying that you are a nice person is not really much value.

So what should a recommendation include? You don't want it to be fluffy, so try to choose ones that are as factual and relevant as possible. Include any or all of these suggestions:

▶ how the person knows you

▶ how they found you to work with

▶ what the working relationship was

▶ some personal traits, such as personable, expert or has integrity

▶ how their business changed as a result of your product or service.

How do you get more recommendations?

It's very simple: ask for them. You may not get them if you don't ask.

You must be connected to the person you are going to ask for a recommendation, so decide who you would like to ask and then get to it. I cover recommendation etiquette in chapter 5 of this book. The great thing that happens over the next few days is that your recommendations start appearing in your inbox and as you read them your self-esteem and confidence soar.

Activity 4

Ask for three recommendations from people you are connected to and have worked with in some way.

Changing your page layout

Did you know you can move certain areas of your page around to change the layout? There's an arrow over in the top right corner of the moveable areas: click and hold it, then drop the section where you want to reposition it. This allows you to position the parts of your profile that you deem the most important as close to the top as possible. If, like me, you have a fair number of recommendations, it can make your page quite long and any information below your recommendations will almost certainly never be seen. By shifting my information around, it's no longer a problem.

Adding your connections

This is the last thing you should do on your page, and only do it when you are completely happy with how your page looks. The first thing your new connections are going to do when they accept your invitation is see what you are up to. If there is nothing there, you may have missed an opportunity.

If you are using Outlook as your mail program you can export your connections (go to 'file', 'export', 'create CSV file'), then from LinkedIn click on 'contacts', 'add connections', then click on the link 'import your desktop email contacts'. If you don't currently use Outlook, simply follow your system's instructions for exporting your contacts into a CSV file. Don't worry at this point that your aunt Mary is on this list: you are simply uploading the file into LinkedIn. Until you decide who to send an invitation to, LinkedIn won't do anything with it.

When it is uploaded, it will tell you who in your contact list is already on LinkedIn, and you can simply choose who to invite by ticking the relevant boxes. Their names will filter into the smaller box on the right side, and then you need to click 'invite selected contacts'.

You can also remove connections from this screen if you ever need to.

Activity 5

Add your email database and see who is already on LinkedIn.

Networking with LinkedIn

Now that you have joined LinkedIn and have a reasonable profile of yourself up for everyone to see, you have to use it. I am sure there are people out there who think that just because they now have a visible profile and a handful of connections, the phone is going to start ringing off the hook. Let me be the bad news bearer on that one: it won't be ringing just yet. You now have to market yourself through the various meeting points within LinkedIn so that others get to meet you and you them. This is largely done by networking within the LinkedIn groups, and getting in touch with your connections' connections.

You may feel a little unsure about where to start, so let's take a look.

Networking with LinkedIn groups

If you type in keywords for the types of groups you would like to look at, a good selection should come up as there are simply thousands and thousands of groups worldwide. An example of this is my search for social media groups: there are 4000 groups just on that topic alone. It does, however, depend on what keywords the group originator put in the group's profile details and title, so you may have to try a few different combinations. I like to add the country in the search terms too, which will bring results that are a little closer to home, but if you are looking to network further afield, you don't need to do this.

Once you have a list of the groups in your industry, there are a few things to point out before you decide to join.

▶ Groups are listed in member number order, so those with the most members will be listed first and they run in descending order. There is very little point in joining a group that has only a handful of people as the discussions will dry up very quickly.

▶ You can see who the group owner is and view their profile.

▶ You can also see how many active discussions there are in that group, and how many jobs have been posted. Look for a good number of discussions rather than nil.

▶ LinkedIn will also automatically offer you a similar group choice for you to look at.

If you click on the title of the group you are interested in, you'll be able to see a little bit more about what the group is about, what to expect from it, who in your network is also a member of it, and any subgroups that run off it. From all of this information you should be able to decide if the group is for you or not: if it is, click 'join group'.

Once you have requested to join the group there may be a vetting process from the group owner or manager, but most groups are automatic entry. The choice is up the owner as there may be competition or certain types of companies or industries that they don't want in their groups.

Activity 6

Use the 'search groups' function to find five relevant groups to join.

When you have been accepted, do abide by any rules that have been set. The rules tend to be the same in most groups:

▶ No promotion of yourself or your services or direct sales pitches.

▶ No spamming of the other group members.

▶ Be respectful of others.

These rules are so everyone can get the same enjoyment and great results from mixing and mingling online.

What should I discuss?

A few tips to get you started:

▶ Make it easy for anyone to contribute.

▶ Encourage a short answer—people are busy.

▶ Respond occasionally; you did start the discussion.

▶ Don't be afraid to dive in and make a start.

People often tell me, 'I don't want to say the wrong thing' or 'I don't have anything worthwhile to say'. This is quite common so you are not on your own.

Even though I work with social media each and every day, I don't very often start conversations about it on LinkedIn as I see that as self-promotion. Instead, I might ask a more general business question such as 'what is your referral process?' or 'what exciting things are happening in your business world at the moment?'.

You see, it's not necessarily about talking shop all the time, but about encouraging other group members to take part and make themselves known, because just like you, they may feel a little self-conscious, but you are all there to network.

Some discussions are started with a statement such as, 'The economy is going down the toilet — here is what I think', but from practice and a bit of monitoring, I find a question will get you a better response. I suppose because you are asking a question, you are really giving a call to action: you are asking someone to answer it, and by our nature, we do like to help others out where we can.

I recently asked a large group, 'What stops you from taking part in or starting a discussion?' and the answers surprised me. Many people were unsure whether they had anything to offer, while others simply wanted to watch, listen and learn. That's an important point to remember if you get a little disappointed when there are not as many comments to your discussion as you would like. Remember there are those silently listening, so you are adding value to someone's business life — you just may not see it at the time.

Another good way of getting others into the discussion is to ask something a little easier to answer and perhaps 'off topic'. For example, the question I had the best response to was, 'What famous person would you like to have a coffee with and why?'. The answers were varied and sometimes surprising. I got over 40 people chatting away and mingling with each other over a very easy question. I would love to know what real business eventually came out of that 'networking event'.

Examples of questions to ask or discussions to start:

▶ What is the worst invention you can think of and why?

▶ What motivates you in business?

▶ What are the best business books you have read?

▶ What is the best thing that is happening in your industry right now?

Another thing to note in the group discussions is that when someone has taken the time to respond to your question, you should follow it up with a comment, even if it is only to say 'thanks for your input'. Remember your manners, just as you would do at a face-to-face networking event when someone has taken the trouble to chip in.

If you find that the group is not for you, you can always up and leave by going to the group settings and clicking the 'leave group' button, but a word of warning: if you leave a group, you can't message any of the group members directly anymore unless you are directly connected to them, and they can't get hold of you as easily either. What I suggest is simply turning off the email alerts by visiting 'my groups' and 'settings'. Then simply uncheck the 'digest email' box so you don't receive any more notifications. That way, you have not left all of those wonderful people forever, you just don't hear from them regularly, and you can always turn them back on.

Creating your own group

Running your own group on LinkedIn is a great way to make new connections, and put yourself forward as a leader in your field, but running a group is a bit like running your website or Facebook page: it's easy to set up, but it needs some time and effort to keep the momentum going and the group growing. It does take a while to get group members engaging, but it is well worth the effort. Once you have a group that is actively starting discussions, and people are actively engaging with each other, that's when relationships are formed, referrals are swapped and deals get done.

Here are some key things to consider when you decide to set up your group.

▶ What is the aim of the group?

▶ Who is going to manage it?

▶ What resources will you use for content?

▶ Who is going to add discussions and news stories?

▶ Who will send consistent announcements out periodically?

▶ What are the guidelines for group participants or the group rules?

What can you do to help your group get up and running? LinkedIn gives you a few templates that you can customise a little, so that you can add in your own flavour about what the group is about and how you run it. The templates include:

▶ a welcome message

▶ a decline message

▶ a 'we are thinking about your application' message.

By personalising each template, you can add all sorts of promotional information and links, so take note of these points and see how you can maximise your own templates:

▶ Include links back to resources in the welcome message template and really maximise the use of the space with useful information, but not spam.

▶ When you set up your group profile, give as much information about the group as possible — what you are trying to achieve, what the purpose of the group is.

▶ Use the group rules section to set clear rules for your group.

▶ Include keywords in the group title and profile that you think people will be searching for when they are looking to join a group.

Send a group message (announcement)

This is a real benefit to running your own group: as the group manager or owner can send the group messages to everyone within the group. It really does give you another database to talk to, but don't abuse it. You don't want your group members leaving in droves because you have overdone the self-promotion.

> ### Tips for sending announcements
>
> Consider these tips before sending announcements:
>
> ■ Send announcements consistently but don't overdo it. You are able to send a message weekly, but monthly is probably the maximum.
>
> ■ Treat your announcement as a newsletter and include resources and value, not just about your company, but other articles too. Make it interesting to as many members as possible.

I have recently had a couple of announcements from one group manager that were really nothing more than a catch-up email containing information about what they had been up to in a business sense, and their trips abroad recently. Now I haven't really got time to be reading other people's long catch-up emails, but I did read them both and it made me wonder if that type of email group announcement was in fact a bright way to correspond. It was a little different after all, so why not give it a go and see?

With all of these social media tools, you have to try it, monitor the response and maybe tweak it to get it right, and then try again.

Manager's Choice

If you have something important to discuss and would like to keep it at the top of the group page for a while, make it Manager's Choice. When you have finished with the topic, un-feature it to move it back down the page and allow something else to be featured.

Growing your group

A bit like getting Facebook fans to 'like' your Facebook page, getting new members to join your group can be frustrating: it just doesn't happen quickly enough. There are a few things you can do to help it along, though:

▶ Send invitations out to others to join your group by clicking on 'invitations' while you are in 'manage group'. This gives you the ability to share the URL of your group and pass it on to others. If you decide to do this, ask your connections to invite their connections in too for a bigger mix of people.

▶ Use one of the three website links on your profile we talked about earlier to invite people to join your LinkedIn group.

▶ Make sure your group description and profile contain the right keywords so that when someone is searching for a group like yours, you come up.

▶ Tweet the group URL and invite others to join.

▶ Add the group link to your website asking others to join.

▶ Add the group link to your email signature.

Activity 7

Review your content plan: what can you add in to help you start and take part in discussions on LinkedIn?

Subgroups

These can be easily set up when the main group gets a little bigger and it will be useful to split up a topic of discussion. For example, if you were to set up a corporate fitness group, your subgroups could be male fitness, female fitness, stress, diet and so on. You can allocate moderators for both subgroups and the main group to keep an eye on what is being said and if there are any discussions that have been flagged by another member for some reason. You can set subgroups up at any time, but I would wait until there are more than around 300 people in your main group: the conversations don't get going with just a few people in there and members may end up leaving if they don't get much value from it.

Setting up your company page

Just as Facebook created its version of a company page, now so has LinkedIn, but the appeal of having a company page on LinkedIn is the professional business-oriented community it sits in.

Normally the profile pages that you set up on LinkedIn are for your own personal use, and it is indeed against LinkedIn's terms and conditions to set up a personal profile page as a business. But LinkedIn has seen that by capturing and promoting more business information in this community, it can make way for a whole lot more engagement and knowledge sharing.

Benefits of a company page

Some benefits of a company page include:

- It's another place to promote your product or service.

- Interested people can 'follow' your company and be notified when you post updates.

- It has a header image to make use of.

- You can link to it from your website.

So, how do you set it up?

Only one person from your company can set up the business page, and you will need to have an email address that matches your domain, so using your Gmail address won't work. This stops others from setting up company pages that they are not authorised to do.

To start your LinkedIn business page, simply click on 'companies' on the top navigation and then 'create a company page'. From there it is fairly self-explanatory and you just need to follow the very easy steps. You can now do the following:

▶ *Set up a showcase page for the main aspects of your business.* This is particularly useful if your brand is known for its sub-brands. For instance, Restaurant Brands could be the company main page, but underneath that will be Starbucks and KFC showcase pages so interested parties can follow the elements of the company that they are particularly interested in.

▶ *Add a careers page if you have vacancies to advertise.* If you are currently looking for new employees, what better place to advertise than on a database with more than 280 million people! The listed vacancy will pop up on the home page of people LinkedIn thinks may be interested and many companies have had success filling vacancies through this method. What is also great is that anyone who clicks on the advertisement can easily see a whole lot more about the company and the other employees who are in their network.

▶ *Follow any company that interests you.* Each time a company that I am following updates something, I am notified on my status update page. How cool is that for inside intelligence, particularly if I am a recruitment agent! I may need help to fill that vacancy that has just been created, or the person that has just been promoted may want to hear from me in their new role.

▶ *See how you are connected to a company.* The company overview page allows you to see how you may be connected to that company: it's a bit of inside intelligence. If you are looking to do business with that company in some way, you may have some inside connections that could possibly be helpful to you, or even pass an introduction message on to the person you need.

▶ *Post your blog posts onto the page.* Let your followers find out more about the company via your company blog posts. Each time you write a new post, post the link to show it on your page.

▶ *Add a disclaimer.* Even if you don't add a disclaimer, make use of this space to write something else.

▶ *Create a new page for a different target audience, which LinkedIn will publish for you, all for free!* If you have a different offering for your US market than for your Canadian market, then the new feature will allow you to create multiple variations of the page, which LinkedIn will automatically show for you. While it doesn't say how many, there seems to be space for six variations.

▶ *Add a button to your website that says 'follow us on LinkedIn'.* Simply copy the HTML code and you're done. You may need your web person to do this bit for you.

Anyone that views your company page also has the option to like, comment on or share the post with their own connections, and if you are the page manager for your company, you have the additional option to feature a post. This keeps the post at the top of your page, which is especially useful if you have an offer or promotion running or simply need to share an important message for some time.

Sponsored updates

LinkedIn has its own advertising platform within LinkedIn enabling you to create ads that you can target to certain criteria. While I am not going to go into too much detail about ads in this book, it is definitely worth spending some time on sponsored updates. The main difference between the two is that the ads appear around the site, usually along the top or down the right-hand side of the page, and as many of them are predominantly just text, I just don't think they are very visible. The sponsored updates, however, are different. These appear within your LinkedIn newsfeed so are much more visible when a connection is scrolling through their news, and you can also use one of your posts as an ad in this way too. To do this, you just need to post your offer or story in the status box as normal, and share. Wait for a minute or so and refresh your page and you should see a 'sponsor update' button appear. From here you can create a campaign and decide exactly who you want to see your ad, and only those people will. This saves you money because the ad is only being shown to relevant eyeballs and not people that don't fit your target criteria. For example, if you just want Business Development Managers in Sydney within the IT industry to see your ad, then you can filter it that low and only pay for those to see it. Likewise, you can keep it as broad as you wish but you will need a large budget! LinkedIn ads and sponsored updates both need playing around with to get the budget and targeting just right and can work for most B2B businesses.

I am sure that this is just the start for LinkedIn's company pages and I suspect that we will see these pages being connected to company groups too, which would be awesome.

Activity 8

Set up your LinkedIn company page and add in your products or services.

Social media success story: Alice @ AtoZ HR

It's always great to hear real-life stories of others who are getting something out of a product or service and so I thought I would share Alice's. Utilising the power of LinkedIn, I posted a status update asking my connections if anyone would like to share their own experiences of LinkedIn and this is how Alice has found using it:

'I have been a member of LinkedIn since 2008. In the beginning I used LinkedIn myself just for fun, to follow people and keep in contact with people I knew already. Business-wise I use LinkedIn for having a quick sneak preview when I am going to meet someone I do not know and to look at their picture in order to recognise them when we meet.

'About two years ago when I was looking for a new career, I used LinkedIn for contacting people in my network. I mailed people that I knew, to meet them at their office and get a feel for their culture. I had conversations with about 20 people in my network from different organisations. But I also wanted to look inside some other organisations where I didn't have any contacts, so I searched for people in my network who knew employees from those companies and I mailed or phoned them. About 50 per cent of my requests were answered positively. After that, I really was inspired! Those conversations gave me the insight to make the choice to become self-employed.

'I took the plunge! Last year I started my own company AtoZ HR (meaning: A-to-Z Human Relations).

'Now I use LinkedIn differently.

'I use LinkedIn for inspiring, marketing, acquisition and relationship management.

- *Inspiring:* Reading news, funny stuff, information about trends in Human Relations and training on LinkedIn inspires me. Furthermore, I follow inspiring people by reading their own posts. This fuels my posts and I pass on this great content to my network.

(continued)

Social media success story: Alice @ AtoZ HR *(cont'd)*

- *Marketing:* When I write a post on my website I leave a comment in a LinkedIn group with a link to my blog and I see in my Google Analytics that people are visiting my website directly from LinkedIn. Furthermore, I am also active in group discussions to help or inspire others with the purpose of triggering people to visit my site or profile and read more about what I can do for them. Instead of giving 'likes' I try to give 'comments' to become more helpful as well as visible.

- *Acquisition:* If I notice that someone I don't know has viewed my profile, I send them an email to thank them and try to connect for opportunities in the future.

- *Relationship management:* LinkedIn is a beautiful tool for relationship management! It is very easy to connect, it is very easy to renew contacts, and it is very easy to make people happy by sending an email after receiving an alert from LinkedIn that someone has a new job or has a birthday.

'I really am an advocate of using LinkedIn, since networking is in my veins and LinkedIn is the best tool to support it!'

Quick tip

Don't be tempted to rush out and invite your entire database just yet. What do you think is the first thing they will do when they receive your invitation? They will want to view your profile, so don't miss this opportunity to shine by having it half-finished. It will let you down.

Conclusion of chapter 3

We have covered quite a lot with LinkedIn in this chapter, so by now you should have an idea of how you will use it effectively for your own business. Your LinkedIn profile is not set in stone, so plan to revisit it in a month to see if you can improve it any more.

In order for you to get some traction with LinkedIn, try to allocate 10 minutes per day to networking online within your chosen groups, and posting status updates.

CHAPTER 4

Twitter basics and using Twitter for your business

Key areas we will cover in chapter 4:

✓ setting up your Twitter account

✓ getting tweeting

✓ using Twitter tools

✓ setting up your listening post.

People ask me all the time, 'Tell me about Twitter, I don't see how it's even of interest to people.' On the surface, you can be forgiven for thinking that, but it can really be a very powerful tool for networking, researching, publishing, icebreaking and listening, so it has many uses. You just need to understand how it works and how to use some of the many tools that are available to help you. In this chapter we will look at some of these tools and share a few more stories about how other companies and individuals have found success with Twitter.

Quick stats www.twitter.com

Here are some interesting Twitter stats:

▶ a quick and easy way to **microblog**

▶ about one billion registered users

▶ 300 billion tweets sent in total

▶ you can tweet on the run

▶ great icebreaker for networking

▶ anyone can do it

▶ 76 per cent of monthly active users access Twitter by a mobile device

What is Twitter?

Twitter was born in 2006. It is based in San Francisco and can be instantly translated from English to 16 other languages, so people all over the world can use Twitter easily—all you need is an internet connection and a device such as a computer or smartphone. It asks the question 'what's happening?' and was originally intended for college kids to keep in touch in a similar way to Facebook, but using only 140 characters, so short and snappy. Others quickly saw the benefits of using this simple system to chat with others around the world, and the phenomenon grew with many millions of people actively 'tweeting' every day.

Businesses then saw the advantages of using such a platform to shout about their products and services. As time progressed and more and more people started tweeting, it became apparent that it could also be used as a listening tool. Individuals saw Twitter as a way to gripe about products or services from large and small brands, a no-holds-barred, out-in-the-open-air conversation. Businesses quickly realised that they needed to do something to keep any bad press about them under control and quickly sort out any issues as they came to light. Likewise, businesses wanted to jump in and listen to all of the positive things that people were saying about their brand and thank them for being cheerleaders. There is also the conversation that is neither positive nor negative, where someone is simply asking a question, such as, 'Who has the better deal, Vodafone or Telstra?' Now if you were either of those companies, you are naturally going to want to engage with that possible customer and convert them to your brand if they are in the market, so Twitter can be used for intelligence too.

Setting up your account

The process is very straightforward: go to www.twitter.com and register, but give some thought to your username. There are some very odd usernames out there and some are very obviously 'get rich quick' schemes or multilevel marketing programs, so don't turn people off with a dumb name. Use either your own name or a version of it if someone else has already taken it, or something associated with your company if it is to be a company account. That might simply be the company name, but as you don't have too many characters to play with, you may need to abbreviate it. Some companies have different accounts for different parts of their business, such as @vodafone_AU and @vodafoneAU_help. They are both part of the same company but have a different voice for the different business aspects they cover.

Home page

This is where you can see how many followers you have, how many you are following yourself, how many tweets you have sent, any tweets you have saved to your favourites, and a whole bunch of other information. It is also where you will see tweets coming in from others that you are following so that you can respond if you want to. You now also have the option of following people that Twitter has suggested: it will suggest people to follow who are 'similar to' the person's profile you are viewing. I must admit, most of the suggested 'who to follow' people have been of interest to me, so a good tool on Twitter's part.

Trending topics is something to keep an eye on also as it shows the hot conversation threads that are going on now. When someone famous dies, there has been a terrorist attack or other big breaking news stories the information is soon out on the Twitter waves for everyone to see and follow without even needing to turn on the TV to find out more.

Profile page

From your profile page you can customise the look and feel of your Twitter page, and add your photo and a bit about yourself. There is also space to put a link back to your website or use it to drive traffic back to your Facebook business page.

If you are an individual setting up your own account, remember your own personal brand is just as important as if you were representing Coca-Cola, so take care. I suggest you have a slightly more relaxed bio than on, say, your LinkedIn page, but still keep it professional. Mine currently says: 'Training and speaking on building and maintaining relationships online. Foody, runner and sometimes cyclist', and I have a link to my Facebook page.

This captures my professional headline that is on all of my branding, with a little extra about my pastimes, which is important when it comes to networking. People do read these profiles, so be sure that what you write is what you are happy to be seen as. I saw one recently that read reasonably professionally but then had 'dirty salsa dancer' at the end. That turned my interest off.

So should you use your company logo or your own picture? Well, people do like to know who they are actually talking to and a logo can come across as a bit too corporate so you have a couple of choices.

▶ Use your own photo with the company-named account.

▶ Use the logo but be sure to make your name known on the profile page so people can talk to you properly. I hate it when I view a profile of someone, and there is simply the company name but no mention of who the person behind it is. How can you communicate with an anonymous person? It gives me an impression of an impersonal company from the start.

When it comes to filling in your location, it's a good idea to put the city as well as the country so that when someone is searching for a business in your city, you come up in the search results. If you just put 'Earth', or 'worldwide', that might be detrimental to your business.

> ### Activity 1
>
> Create your profile for Twitter. Keep it professional with a relaxed feel.

Finding followers and who to follow

Now that you have built your Twitter page and added some information to it by way of a photo and a short bio, you are ready to find some interesting people to follow and get some followers back. By the general rule of reciprocity, many people that you follow will in fact follow you back. Start off by seeing who you know from your address book in the 'find friends' link, which you can find on your home page just under 'who to follow'. That will bring up a search box so you can simply type in either their Twitter username, if you know it, or their full name. If they are listed on Twitter, it should pop up for you and you just need to make your choice and click on the follow button. You can also export and upload your contacts from Gmail, Yahoo!, Hotmail and AOL or invite via email.

What Twitter itself doesn't give you is a real way to search a directory for new people to follow. You can click on 'who to follow' and browse by interests or find friends, and a list will be created for you. Take a look at www.twellow.com, which is almost a Twitter directory as it covers just about everyone you could possibly want to follow. You should register your own details with the site (normally just your Twitter username and password) and then fill out a few details about who and where you are so that others can find you. Then get searching.

Search for businesses in your area, your prospects, clients and people of interest to you and add them in. As I said earlier, most people will automatically follow you back unless you look like a possible spam account.

Activity 2

Search for and follow your first 50 people. Some of them will follow you back. If you search and follow more than 50 in one hit, you may be flagged as a spam robot.

Spam and abuse

You will notice your Twitter followers drop off by quite a chunk occasionally as Twitter culls the spam accounts out, so don't be too concerned if you see yours take a nosedive one day. Twitter is pretty good at keeping the rubbish down. It is probably worth mentioning at this stage that it is not wise to become a spam account yourself, as your life on Twitter will be short. By spam account, I mean setting up your account to target people with the sole purpose of pushing your product or service continually. You may find your account deactivated.

Here are a few activities that may draw some attention to you and should be avoided:

▶ aggressive following in large numbers

▶ creating large numbers of accounts

▶ sending large numbers of **@replies**

▶ having a small number of followers compared with the number you are following

▶ attempting to sell followers

▶ using pornography anywhere.

These are just a few; a full list of the dos and don'ts can be found on Twitter under 'help'.

Get tweeting

The next step is to decide what you are trying to get out of Twitter and work on a plan to get you there. Whatever you are trying to achieve, there are some basic principles that remain the same.

▶ *Add value, don't sell.* Nobody likes to be sold to, so gain people's trust and respect by sending out interesting article links about your field of expertise. Don't send these out from your own website every time; vary them from other respectable sites too. I suggest two in 10 should be from your own business sites.

▶ *Retweet (RT).* Retweeting items that you have found interesting that someone else has posted says two things. It tells the originator of the tweet that you found it interesting, and that it is likely to be interesting to your followers. Retweeting is the ultimate compliment on Twitter and great exposure for you as that person tweets the information on to their networks too. Can you imagine if someone in their network also RT'd it and on it goes? Where would your post end up? That is the exponential effect of Twitter.

▶ *Engage.* Let's say you would like to meet the CEO of a particular company but at this stage he doesn't even know you exist. Apart from calling him on the phone or calling in at his place of work, how else are you going to get in touch with him? See if he is on Twitter with the search function, add him to a list so that you don't miss his tweets, and when you see a tweet from him that you can engage with, say something. Now it doesn't need to be earth shattering or thought provoking, just the start of building up a rapport. If he has just tweeted that he is walking his Doberman to the park to watch his young son play in a soccer tournament this afternoon, you might simply ask about his dog as you have a Doberman too, or wish the boy good luck—it was your son's tournament last weekend. The CEO will more than likely reply with thanks at the very least, and now he knows you exist. Don't blow it now by jumping in feet first; court him with chit-chat and interesting links about his industry. It might take a little time, so don't rush in and ruin it. When the time is right, meet for a coffee and you will feel like you already know him. It makes it a warm call rather than a cold one, and a great way to network online.

▶ *Grow*. You need to actively grow your followers so that you create a tribe of people that see you as the expert in your field, and add value to their world. When you do then publish something from your own business, more people will have the opportunity to see it, which is more exposure for you. Think back to the exponential effect of Twitter and where your post could possibly end up.

▶ *Listen*. Use Twitter to listen to what people are saying about you or your brand.

Activity 3

Send a tweet and find something of interest that you can retweet.

Communicating on Twitter

There are two ways to communicate on Twitter—@replies and direct messages (DM). @replies are directed to a particular person on Twitter and they view the messages in their @replies or mentions column, but anyone else can see them on the web too. Think about it as shouting across a football pitch to your mates on the other side with everyone else in between listening in. Direct messages are a bit more private with only the two parties able to see the message, just like an email. The proviso is that you must be following each other for a DM to work in the first place. With @replies, even though they are visible via search, only the person you are replying to actually sees the tweet in their stream, so if you want everyone else to see the reply as well as the individual, make sure the @ sign is not the very first letter. For example, 'Have a lovely weekend@richardbranson' will mean that Richard will see it and so will all your other followers without having to search. A reply of just '@richardbranson have a lovely weekend' will only be seen by him (or probably more likely his social media team).

If you are using an application such as Tweetdeck or Hootsuite to sort your tweets rather than Twitter itself, you will see direct messages in one column and mentions (@replies) in another when you set it up, so you shouldn't miss any. Direct messages will also filter through into your ordinary email inbox as a duplicate unless you turn it off in your Twitter settings.

Twitter terms

You'll need to know the following terms to communicate on Twitter:

- @replies are messages to you but visible to all.

- DMs (direct messages) are messages to you that only you can see.

- RT (retweets) are tweets that have been passed on, seen as interesting.

- # (**hashtags**) allow you to follow a conversation about a particular topic. For example #Budget2014, or #tsunami. Simply click on the hashtag to follow the whole conversation.

Lists

Lists are a great way to file the people you are following so that you can keep track of important tweets coming in without them getting lost in the flow of things. When you start getting into the hundreds and thousands of followers, it is impossible to see and respond to them all. You can create lists for anything you want to filter out such as clients, prospects, competition, motivational, educational and so on. That means that once you have added someone to a list you have created, their tweets will simply filter through to that list for you to see easily and respond to if you wish. I find this particularly helpful for monitoring business prospects and my current clients.

A word of warning, though: when you create your lists Twitter's default is to make the list public, which means that anyone, following you or not, can click on your list of clients, and see who they all are, and do the same thing with your prospects too. The thing to do with these lists is to change the default to private. Tweetdeck (which we'll look at later in this chapter) works exactly the opposite way around, with private as the default, which is much safer.

There is no reason why you need to keep your entire lists private, but just be cautious with any sensitive lists that you have created such as your client list.

Advanced and auto following tools

As your account grows, it can become a little tedious clicking on each new follower's message and deciding if you want to follow that person or not and actioning it, so there are tools that will do it automatically for you. That way, you can still see the emails of who is following you, but you don't need to actually do anything with them. Incidentally, you can turn these email alerts off in your Twitter settings too if you wish, but I like to be nosey and monitor them. The tool to automate your followers is www.socialoomph.com, and you can do a whole heap of other things there too to automate Twitter. There is even the option to send an auto response message to someone when they follow you. I used to use it, but I think it looks a little like spam, as it is not personalised in any way and comes across as auto-generated, which of course it is. Your choice, the option is there.

Advanced search

Go to www.twitter.com/search-advanced, and you can look for a whole bunch of variables, such as location, conversations between certain people and dates of conversations past. This is particularly handy if you are, say, a catering company and you are looking for people planning events who are in need of caterers in a certain city. There are many things you could search for and this is a great and easy-to-use tool to add to your toolbox. Give it a go and see what you can find out that is useful to your business.

Tweetdeck and Hootsuite

These are probably the most used applications that run with Twitter, as they make it so simple to keep tabs on things all on one screen. There are others that do a similar job, but www. tweetdeck.com and www.hootsuite.com are my favourites. So what makes them so special? You can:

▶ view all of your incoming tweets in one column

▶ see your @replies on the same page

▶ see your direct messages on the same page

▶ update your personal Facebook page from here

▶ update your LinkedIn status update, company page and groups from here

▶ add several accounts you may be managing, all on one screen

▶ set up search result columns so you don't miss important tweets.

Depending on which one you opt for, you can allow multiple users to update multiple channels all at the same time, which is useful for time management as well as security.

The software is free and sits on your desktop or smartphone. You can see why I like it as it offers so much in one place. I simply open it up in the morning, and it sits in the background all day for me to check on periodically, and with the columns clearly set out, I can see when a client or a prospect has tweeted or I have a message. Once it is set up you can spend as much or as little time as you like on it each day.

Activity 4

Set up Tweetdeck or Hootsuite and familiarise yourself with it.

Table 4.1 shows some handy Twitter tools.

Table 4.1: handy Twitter tools

Site	Web address	Use
Tweetdeck	www.tweetdeck.com	Create columns for ease
Hootsuite	www.hootsuite.com	Similar to Tweetdeck
Search	www.twitter.com/search-advanced	Search for a subject or name
Twellow	www.twellow.com	Yellow Pages of followers
SocialOomph	www.socialoomph.com	Auto follow, auto reply
Social Mention	www.socialmention.com	Set up alerts
Google Alerts	www.google.com/alerts	Set up alerts
Twitter Grader	www.twittergrader.com	How influential are you on Twitter?
Tweepi	www.tweepi.com	Clean out your twitter account
Friend or Follow	www.friendorfollow.com	See who is not following you back

Listening out for your brand

As people are now taking to online channels to chat in public, have you thought about what they may be saying about your brand? Twitter is a great tool for listening to conversations people are having within Twitter. Listening to what people are saying about your brand makes sense. If someone has something negative to say about you or your brand, wouldn't you like to know about it so you can respond? Following are a couple of examples of what I mean.

Real example: get it right — coffee shop

One summer's day I had a bit of spare time in between appointments, so I headed to the nearest coffee shop for a sit-down and a well-earned coffee. I placed my order, and took a seat on one of the sofas to watch the world go by down on the waterfront. The sun was streaming in through the windows on a beautiful day, with tourists from all four corners of the world enjoying the day.

As I sat waiting for my drink, my mind wandered from the outside world to what was happening in the coffee shop, or rather what hadn't been happening in the coffee shop. As I took in what I was looking at, I thought I must have been imagining things. The shop front was pretty much glass all the way along, and with the summer sun streaming through it, I could really see just how dirty and smeared the windows were. Now I am not a particularly fussy person when it comes to clean windows, but these were so dirty and smeary that it really did shock me. After all, it was a coffee shop, a place where they serve drinks and food, and so to have filthy windows is simply not on.

The coffee shop in question was also part of a large national chain with many coffee shops throughout the country, so you tend to expect a little more than what I was looking at from a reputable brand.

I decided to tweet about it, so I got my iPhone out of my bag and proceeded to tweet where I was, who the coffee chain was and what was bothering me. Within a couple of minutes, one of my followers came back to me and said that they had been in the same coffee shop a couple of days earlier and they too had noticed the same thing, so I wasn't the only one who thought it was below average.

(continued)

Real example: get it right—coffee shop *(cont'd)*

That now made two tweets out there talking about this particular brand's premises in a not-so-flattering way, and others could potentially join in if they were listening and had something to add, but on this occasion, no-one else did.

I thought no more about it as I finished my drink and went to my next appointment, which was a speaking engagement for a client's networking evening, so it was not until a couple of hours later that I received my telephone message left by the CEO of the coffee company. My first thought was, 'Oh my goodness, what have I done?' as I dialled his number. 'What hornets' nest might I have stirred up?'

He was very pleasant and explained that he had seen my tweet and also seen the follow-up tweet from the other person, and was concerned about my experience not being a great one in the coffee shop down the street. He explained that the management of the shop had recently changed and that there were some problems with the glass not being able to be cleaned properly. They were even in discussions with the landlord of the building to see if they could get the glass changed, it was that much of an issue. He assured me they were working on a solution and that my experience was not what he wanted to happen. What else could he do to put matters right?

I wasn't after gift vouchers or anything like that, I just wanted a coffee in a clean environment, but my point is this: he was listening, and he acted swiftly to see how he could help. For that, I give the brand top marks. If the company had simply ignored those first tweets, it might have escalated into something bigger as Twitter makes it very easy to shout about things, both good and bad.

I asked him how he had seen the tweet so quickly and he said he had alerts set up on his phone, so again top marks for taking an active approach to listening to what is being said about his brand.

Real example: beware of impersonators — HJ Heinz

Back in 2009 Michael decided to see what would happen if he impersonated a big brand on Twitter. He wanted to find out how long he could keep it up for before the brand realised they were being impersonated, and what action they would then take. The only criteria for his choice of brand were that they were extremely well known globally, that he had an interest in their brand as he used it himself, and that they didn't already have a social media presence.

He picked on Heinz.

So on 1 December 2009 he set up a Twitter page called @HJ_Heinz, branded it with the Heinz ketchup bottle for a logo, and added a profile informing followers that they could expect news, recipes and information about Heinz, and set to work tweeting and getting new followers.

He tweeted interesting information off the Heinz website and added links to recipes and anything else he found of interest, but at no time was he ever malicious — that was never the plan. He made sure he was cautious at all times, as he was representing a huge global brand. From there, he had to gain followers organically, so he started to search for people who had already mentioned Heinz in their tweets, and followed them.

He also targeted tweeters from the Pittsburgh area, as Heinz is a big part of the community there. It didn't take long to get more than 350 followers, but on 14 December 2009 his account name was changed and he was no longer allowed to carry on as @HJ_Heinz. Twitter notified him that the account was in breach of the Twitter rules and so could not continue as it was, and he was also told to take the logo off the page. The name of the account was then changed to @NOTHJ_Heinz. He states in an article about his experiment that no-one from Heinz ever got in touch with him, which was disappointing.

(continued)

Real example: beware of impersonators —
HJ Heinz *(cont'd)*

Michael never at any time tried to be malicious; it was simply an experiment to him to see if he could get away with it, which he did for two weeks. So was Heinz really listening every day?

My opinion is that they can't have been, otherwise they would surely have seen the fake account and done something sooner. But another question might be why did they not see Michael as a true fan and see if they could work together in some capacity? He was after all a loyal fan: what better cheerleader does a company need?

This story of how Heinz got caught out is from some time ago but it's still very relevant to many smaller companies today because it's a huge lesson in listening in the right places. You don't hear of big well-known brands coming up against this sort of thing anymore because, thankfully, they are now all listening and doing something about it if an issue does arise.

Listening online — setting up alerts

So what sort of things should you be listening for and where should you be listening? Twitter is a great place to start, followed by Social Mention, Tweetdeck and Google Alerts, which are simply alerts that are delivered to your inbox about a given keyword such as your company name (these are explained further on). I have set alerts up for Linda Coles, Blue Banana, Blue Bananas, Bluebanana20 and a few others. As most of my social media usernames are bluebanana20 (I wasn't quick enough to get Blue Banana), I watch out for both because people often simply refer to me as Blue Banana, and I don't want to miss what they are saying. The problem with this is that I get everything to do with Blue Banana the clothing and body-piercing company. Some of those piercing tweets make my eyes water!

It is an easy job to monitor once you have the systems in place and it only takes me a few seconds a day to filter through the Blue Banana tweets as I've learned to recognise who is who.

You can also listen to what your competitors are saying, even without them knowing that you are listening in, so that may be useful in your industry. I used to do this, but found I was spending time worrying about what they were up to rather than concentrating on my own business. If you want to follow someone in your industry, follow someone who you admire and can learn from, which is far more positive, and probably more worthwhile.

To set a Google Alert, set up a Google account if you don't have one already, and click on 'alerts' or go to www.google.com/alerts. Depending on how often you want to be informed, you can set the email notifications to as it happens, daily or weekly, so you can control the number of emails coming in.

If you are watching a search term rather than a word, you will need to put the 'speech marks' around the term, so, for example, if I want to watch out for Blue Banana, I will need to enter 'Blue Banana', otherwise I will get alerts with just blue or just banana in them, which is a bit of a waste of time and far too labour-intensive. You can set up as many alerts as you wish, and see which ones are of value to you.

Activity 5

Set up your Google Alerts using the keyword ideas in the box in the next section.

Keywords to monitor

Keywords to monitor include:

- your name
- your name spelled incorrectly
- your company name
- your company abbreviated
- your competitors
- your industry
- topics of interest.

Listening with Tweetdeck

With Twitter, there are a few ways to monitor tweets, but I find that simply using Tweetdeck and setting up separate columns for each search term is enough. That way, the tweet is quickly filtered out from the mainstream and is visibly sitting there in its own column waiting for me to notice it. If you download Tweetdeck to your smartphone, you can see the tweets coming through while you are on the move. Again, see which terms you need to monitor as you may find too many a bit of a headache.

The columns can also be used for listening to specific people within your industry or to those who you are interested in that you simply want to snoop on.

I also have columns and alerts set up for areas that I want to respond to such as 'looking for a speaker' or 'social media webinar', so I can respond to someone's request quickly. You might do the same for your business. If you are a florist, you might look out for 'florist in Sydney'. Think about what someone tweeting about needing a florist would enter if they're in Sydney—probably something like 'can anyone recommend a florist in Sydney?' That would then get picked up and filtered into your column for you to see and pounce on. This is a simple way to use tweets to generate a little extra business.

twitter.com/search-advanced gives you the same functionality as Tweetdeck, but you also have the ability to define the area. As Urgent Couriers found out, having a Tweetdeck column set up for 'need a courier' meant that the filter would also pick up tweets from the other side of the world, which was not a lot of good to it. By using twitter.com/search-advanced, it can restrict it to a 100 km radius of Auckland. Much better for its business and it also cuts out the irrelevant tweets.

Activity 6

Set up your alerts on Tweetdeck with the ideas in the keywords box.

Real example: Urgent Couriers

Urgent Couriers was interviewed on national TV about how it has generated business using Twitter and, in particular, using the listening tools to help people out. It has also used it to build up its client base by networking on Twitter, simply chatting to other local businesspeople and building a relationship, just like you would offline.

It also has columns set up to filter out its clients' tweets as well as its prospects' tweets so it can keep up to date with what is going on in their businesses too.

In order to measure its success with spending time on Twitter, it has set up a specific email address so that any emails coming into the company at that address can be tracked back to the success of its Twitter presence. Great idea!

Real example: Telecom

Some time ago I was asked if I would be willing to speak at a luncheon for young businesspeople on social media, but it was to be a little different in that it was purely questions and answers over lunch. Not a large gathering, just about 20 people in a private room, which sounded great. I went along on the day, and mixed and mingled with the majority of the guests, but it's hard to get to say hello to everyone, so inevitably there were people I missed out. After the lunch was over and I returned to my office, I checked Tweetdeck as a matter of course, and there were a couple of tweets in my 'Linda Coles' column but I did not recognise who the person was that had tweeted them. I clicked on her profile and noticed that she worked for one of New Zealand's top five companies and was simply saying that she had enjoyed the lunch and discussion topic of LinkedIn with me.

Now she had made the effort to post that, so it warranted a response at the very least, which I did by simply saying something like, 'Glad you found it useful, have a great afternoon'. From that initial conversation on Twitter, we exchanged a handful more tweets over a period of a couple of weeks, and when a complimentary slot became available on a LinkedIn workshop I was running, I offered it to her. To my surprise and delight, she accepted, which meant I was then able to meet her in person and say hi properly.

As time went on, one of her colleagues asked me if I would like to write an article for a new e-magazine that they were launching to all of their business customers in the coming weeks, so obviously I jumped at the chance and our professional relationship has continued to grow.

My point here is that without listening for possible tweets, I would never have picked hers up as she had used my name and not my Twitter username. From there, I gently kept the conversation going, which resulted in her attending a workshop I was running so she was able to see the depth of my knowledge on the subject and then pass my details on to a colleague for the article submission.

To be able to work with one of the country's top five companies is a real honour and would have been almost impossible without the use of Twitter.

Social media success story: Misha's Vineyard Wines

Misha Wilkinson is the owner and director of Misha's Vineyard Wines and first started using social media back in 2005, when LinkedIn was pretty much the only site available to network on. She then signed up with Facebook in 2008, so still before many of us really even knew what social media was. From there, Misha's Vineyard has gone from strength to strength with different platforms, but she is amazed at how successful Twitter has been. When it first started off, like many businesses, she didn't have any sort of social media plan, just the 'stick your toe in' mentality, but that has since changed. You really do need to understand where you are taking your brand so that you can easily travel down that road.

Here is a great story that Misha sent to me for this book, and a fine example of how she uses Twitter. I will leave it to her to tell you the story.

'My husband had to make a trip to the US and thought while he was there it would be good to make some preliminary contacts in the wine sector, although we hadn't planned to distribute our wine in the US until the following year, so hadn't done serious research into the market. I had just joined up to Twitter, and by luck my Twitter "mentor" was a guy who owns a very high-end US restaurant. I told him we needed some wine contacts and told him in what areas, and he tweeted to his community of friends what we were looking for. In turn some of those people retweeted to their communities.

(continued)

Social media success story: Misha's Vineyard Wines *(cont'd)*

'Pretty soon I was having chats on Twitter with wine retailers, potential distributors, and sommeliers based in the US. A number of appointments were scheduled (on Twitter) and my husband duly went to the US and met up with these contacts. The process of finding all these contacts on Twitter took three days and it resulted in several business meetings in the US. It proved the fastest way to "network" and set up business meetings that I've ever encountered.

'Wine is something people like to share and talk about. The great thing about Twitter is that wine lovers take photos of the bottles they have enjoyed. Several times there have been photos of our bottles of wine shared on Twitter—mainly by enthusiastic consumers. You can see these messages (using the simple search tools on Twitter) and you can thank the person for their positive tweet and the photo of your wine bottle or label.

'The enjoyment that a consumer gets to have a vineyard owner make contact with them and thank them for their comments is enormous! It pushes a positive review to a positive relationship with the wine brand. We all know that word-of-mouth is a great way to spread information, especially for wine, and Twitter is just electronically assisted word-of-mouth. But it actually works better as it's written not spoken (so the message doesn't get changed as it gets passed on) and it's much much faster. The other benefit is you can listen in on all the word-of-mouth recommendations that are going on. Great feedback.'

'Misha explains how they use the tools available to promote their product:

- *Developing media relationships*. We have developed one-to-one relationships with wine journalists around the world—some of whom have specifically visited us when coming to NZ. Instead of just a formal contact with a journalist, relationships can be built with more informal and regular contact. And it works both ways—we know the journalist better and they find out more about us. We have had increased media coverage in traditional media through the media contacts made through social media.

- *Making business contacts.* We have been able to connect with wine distributors and wine retailers in several countries, which has resulted in increasing our network of contacts in potential export markets. My social media community has suggested names of potential importers and distributors, as well as introductions to them, and some serious business meetings and discussions have subsequently been set up.

- *Increasing wine reviews.* When wines are reviewed, I circulate the review to the social media community—and many of them then circulate it to their respective communities. All of this increases the likelihood of people wanting to try your wine as more people hear of you and read a positive review! There have been many times when someone in my community has read a positive review I've sent out and then told me they bought the wine to try as a result. They then send out their comments—which so far have always been positive! There is a close correlation with someone with whom you've made contact with on Twitter and then their interest in wanting to try your wine...because they "know you". A regular question we receive after an interaction through social media is, "Where can I buy your wines?".

- *Increasing website traffic.* Our primary platform is still our website as it's a 100 per cent exclusive platform for our brand and it's where people learn more about us. Social media vehicles drive hits to our website each day as when we post new blogs on our website, or upload the latest wine reviews or press releases, all the links we send out on Twitter and Facebook take people to our website.

(continued)

Social media success story: Misha's Vineyard Wines *(cont'd)*

- *Increasing trade awareness.* We have one-to-one Twitter and Facebook relationships with many restaurants, wine retailers and sommeliers, which is invaluable. It increases the awareness and knowledge of our brand. And then when you develop an ongoing interaction with these people, it increases preference for your brand. This concept of creating awareness then knowledge then preference for a brand is the basis of any marketing communications campaign—with social media you can achieve all three brand-building activities.

- *Conducting research and competitor analysis.* Seeing what other wineries do, locally and overseas, provides useful competitive analysis. It allows you to benchmark your activities with wineries elsewhere. Social media also allows the ability to understand what the latest trends are—what are wine bloggers blogging about? What wines are restaurants putting on the lists? What wines and styles are consumers talking about?

- *Enabling a brand check.* With vehicles like Twitter, you can search on your brand name and find out who is talking about you—is it positive or negative? Then you can respond to them directly—to turn a negative into a positive or to thank them for a positive comment.

- *Enabling development of communities.* Through the use of hashtags when using Twitter, you can enable all messages to be collated so that the "community" of tweeters can see all messages with a certain tag. This enables sharing of information, regardless of location, and allows information to be shared in real time. An example of this was all New Zealand wineries were encouraged to use #nzwineharvest in all tweets about the 2010 harvest. This allowed every winery in NZ to share information on their harvest and develop camaraderie across the country during the harvest. Photos and videos were shared as well as information on the harvest itself. It was also the perfect place for wine media to get a real-time look at what the 2010 harvest was like—by hearing directly from the wineries. Not only were journalists interested, but all the wine trade, sommeliers, wine consumers and so on. Another example is with Facebook. We posted photos of harvest with all the crew that worked on our vineyard. They were able to go to our Facebook page and 'tag' their photos (that is, put their names on them). They then appeared on their own Facebook pages so their communities could see the photos and share in their experience of doing the harvest with their friends and family.

The way I would describe social media platforms like Twitter and Facebook is that it's like being at a trade show all day every day. But with social media platforms, it doesn't cost anything to be there—and you don't get sore feet! You are virtually at your stand saying things about your products and your brand, and sometimes the odd comment about things in general. Some people will walk by, and some stop for a quick chat—and some want to make arrangements to meet you. Some people who like what they see and hear will come back again and again, and bring their friends with them to meet you. Having a social media presence gives you a virtual participation in a worldwide tradeshow.'

Misha's advice to others who are still thinking about using social media includes:

- 'Get a social media "mentor"—that is, someone who is using social media now and has some "tricks of the trade" they can pass on.

- Don't waste any time! This is a complete no-brainer—for most businesses anyway'.

Conclusion of chapter 4

Twitter can be used for many different business tasks as well as keeping up to date with your interests, but at least set it up as a listening post and check in regularly to see what, if anything, is being said about you or your brand.

Each day, spend five minutes in the morning posting relevant and interesting information, and revisit Twitter in the afternoon to see if you have any replies that need attention.

Your content plan will come in very handy when using Twitter so make sure you have filled in all of the boxes.

CHAPTER 5

Online etiquette and preserving your reputation

Key areas we will cover in chapter 5:

✓ getting your content right

✓ you've connected—now what?

✓ keeping in touch with your connections

✓ applying your good manners

✓ playing the name game.

It might seem a little obvious that you need to behave online as you would in person, but for some reason we sometimes see the two differently and so act differently. Let's have a look at some of the things we can do to make sure we don't upset anyone.

Getting your content right

Everything you post online stays there forever and is a direct reflection on you, so beware of posting things that you wouldn't want your mother to see! You don't have to write everything yourself, but at least be aware of the whole content of what you are posting if it is an article from another source, and always include the link to the original article. That way, the rightful owner of the content gets the attribution. Remember 'you are what you share'.

Working with original content

So where will your content come from? Once you have started your social media plan from chapter 1, you should have a clear understanding of what your social media efforts are going to achieve for you.

Your content will come from:

▶ *personal content*—your own efforts from articles, videos and blog posts

▶ *third-party content*—respected industry online publications. The emphasis here is on respected, professional and interesting content.

When it comes to third-party content, it is important you don't simply copy the article onto your own blog or Facebook page and make it your own, as you could find yourself in trouble for a copyright breach. It is, however, perfectly acceptable to mention what the article is about and link back to the original article so that the original author gets the attribution.

Install a spellcheck tool

Another very important thing I would like to share with you is to install a spellchecker in your browser bar if you don't already have one. Go to www.google.com/toolbar and download one free of charge. You will need this if you use Internet Explorer, but Mozilla and some of the other browsers have one built in.

You will be amazed at how many times you make a mistake and need to correct it. Remember, first impressions count, so don't let all of your hard work be undone by spelling mistakes. It's probably worth mentioning not to rely on it 100 per cent, as some autocorrect words will still be wrong.

Making connections with LinkedIn

Very few people ignore you in real-life face-to-face networking situations. So why do they do so online? The simple answer is because they probably don't even realise that they are! There are many things that we do online that we just wouldn't dream of doing in person, so let's go through a few key areas to really make sure you stand out for being a pleasure to know online.

Think about whether you follow up every LinkedIn connection request you get. Many people simply click 'accept', and think no more of it. When someone requests to connect with you and you simply click 'accept', and then make no effort to carry on the conversation, you are simply saying hello and the conversation stops dead there. The only thing you gain by doing this is a string of connections that don't have any real value: you become a connection collector, and you wouldn't do it while face-to-face networking; that would simply be rude.

So how can you use social etiquette to really make your LinkedIn connections valuable and to stand out from the crowd at the same time? I suggest you view LinkedIn as your own boardroom of connections versus your coffee-shop connections on Twitter or Facebook. Your connections on LinkedIn tend to be managers, directors, business owners, CEOs and the like, and could be a very different set of connections from those on your Facebook page.

Send personalised connection requests

When you first send a possible contact an invitation on LinkedIn, do it from their profile page by clicking the 'connect' button.

We will use Paul as an example. By adding Paul this way rather than simply going to the 'add connections' tab, you can send a personalised message, such as, 'Thanks for the coffee yesterday, it was great to catch up'. This gives you the opportunity to remind Paul where you know him from, which is particularly useful if you're getting back in touch after a long period of time, such as with someone from an old job or your school days.

If you simply send a connection request from the 'add connections' box, there is no facility to personalise your message, so avoid this where possible. It might be a quick and easy way to add a handful of new connections, but spend the time and do it right by adding your personal touch to each one individually.

Reply when accepting a connection request

All too often I receive the standard email from LinkedIn that says a connection request has been accepted, but I rarely then get a short message from the new connection at least saying 'hi'.

When Paul has accepted my connection request, he could then send a short message back. I like to take a look at my new connection's profile if I am not too familiar with them, and find something I can comment on. That may be something like he comes from my home town, or works for a company I know well, or perhaps I can see from his interests that he too is a cyclist. Whatever it may be, try and find something to start a short conversation to build on your relationship together: make the effort to find out more, just like you would in person.

Activity 1

Go to your LinkedIn page and search for connections that you admire within your industry. Are you able to connect with them? Are they in a group with you?

I've covered a couple of the initial and basic steps we tend to forget about, so now let's look at composing a message to a group of our connections.

Keep in touch with your connections

You can send a message to only 50 people at any one time and this is a good thing, otherwise I am sure you would see a lot of spam, but there are a couple of things to note here:

▶ *Your opening*. If you're sending an email to a group of connections, think about your greeting. How are you going to address them? I suggest you start with something like 'Hi everyone' or 'Greetings to you all' and then immediately say 'Please excuse my lack of personalisation in this email as I am sending this out to a group of connections'. That way, you can be forgiven and you have addressed any possible bad-manners critics.

▶ *Hide others' emails*. Always uncheck the box that says 'allow recipients to see each other's email address'. This then makes it a BCC (blind carbon copy): you are protecting other people's privacy by not sharing their email address with everyone else. When you receive a message yourself this way, respond if the content is relevant to you. If the sender has followed the rules in the next section about message content and what to add, hopefully you did find something of interest.

Consider your message content

If you want your connections to leave you in droves, then feel free to write about all the good things you do or can offer from your company! I have made this mistake in the past myself and then I came to my senses. I realised I needed to treat this form of communicating just the same way as my newsletters — that is, by adding valuable resources. People don't want to hear about you all the time and what you can offer, but they do want to know about how you could possibly help fix one of their problems.

A recent example of an email to my connections looked like figure 5.1 (overleaf).

Figure 5.1: example email to connections

Hi everyone,

Please excuse the lack of personalisation on this message as it is coming to you through LinkedIn.

I wanted to let you all in on three pieces of information that may be of use to your business in the very near future.

The first thing I wanted to share is a book I am reading called *The Referral Engine: Teaching Your Business to Market Itself* by John Jantsch. It is a superb, easy-to-read book, packed full of things to do to increase your referrals. One to keep hold of and refer back to time and again.

You may also be interested that XXX and XXX have partnered together for an event and Jack Daly the Sales & Sales Management guru will perform a free 45-minute webinar this Wednesday 30th June at 1pm.

If you are interested I have attached the registration link below, please also feel free to pass on to any other contacts that you feel may benefit.

Jack is a great speaker with a huge amount of knowledge when it comes to sales, so don't miss it. He will also be here in person on July 30th for a full day seminar.

Here is the link XXXXXXXXX

Finally, this company is giving some of the large stationery retailers a run for their money with pricing. Take a look at XXXXXXXX

That's about it for passing on a bit of useful information; I hope you find some, if not all of it, of use.

Kind regards,

Linda, Blue Banana

Nowhere in there is there anything about my company, simply three bits of information I thought would be great to pass on. It contained a great book that most businesses could probably utilise, a free event being put on by two great companies and a website that may save a business a bit of money.

By keeping in touch this way, my aim is simply to add value but, at the same time, to put myself back on the radar of my connections.

Activity 2

Create your own message that you could send out to your connections, taking care not to make it all about you.

Ask for recommendations

Recommendations are a valuable part of your LinkedIn profile and could be the one thing that gets you the deal when a possible client is comparing you with your competitor. Most people only have a couple of recommendations so you can stand out from the crowd with a good number of genuine and applicable recommendations. A good number to aim for is 10.

You will notice that the recommendation request form is another auto-generated template, so it needs personalising: you will need to personalise both the body of the message and the subject line. I like to change mine to read something like 'Recommendation request' as the subject line and 'Are you able to write a recommendation about the presentation I did for your company last week?' in the main body. Don't make the request too long, but be clear on what you want a recommendation for.

If you are asking Paul for a recommendation about a seminar he attended that you spoke at, you could change the message to say 'I hope you enjoyed the seminar last week. If you feel that you are able to write a brief recommendation about how you found my presentation and speaking skills, I would appreciate it. I totally understand if you would prefer not to. Kind regards ...'

There is no need to open your message with 'Dear ...', as LinkedIn will automatically add that in for you by choosing from the drop-down box.

In a nutshell, you should look at personalising every aspect of LinkedIn that you can, making each and every standard template your own. It may take you a little longer, but the value you'll get from doing the job right will far outweigh the effort.

Ask yourself, if you were meeting face to face, what would you be doing differently? People easily judge on first impressions, so make yours a great one, each and every time you connect.

Applying good manners to Facebook

So what about etiquette for Facebook? I asked fellow speaker, author and trainer Kevin Knebl what he thinks about social media etiquette for both business and pleasure. Kevin spends his days educating companies both big and small on the benefits of using social media and being social to one another. This is what he said:

••

'Facebook is the world's largest high school reunion. When I graduated from high school in 1982, back when the Earth was cooling, I had a little black book that contained my girlfriend's phone number and the phone numbers of some of my drinking buddies. As of this writing, there are over one billion people on Facebook. That's a lot of people. A heck of a lot of people. If Facebook were a country, it would be the third-largest country on Earth, right behind China and India and ahead of the US. Facebook isn't a mood ring, pet rock or hula hoop. It's been here a long time with no sign of leaving: it's growing every day.

'Communication platforms are always changing. I'm sure that the telephone was a real shocker for the smoke signal and two cans and a string set. Facebook is the current state-of-the-art tool in terms of communication platforms. And that's an important point: it's a communication channel. In a more and more interconnected, over-caffeinated, hyper-competitive, 24/7/365 world, Facebook is a great way to stay in touch with huge numbers of people, take the pulse of society and generally keep in contact with the world.

'The paradox is that while we're all connecting online, there is not a lot different about our communication styles. I often have people ask me after my speaking engagements, "How should

I be online?" My answer is usually, "Well, unless you have a multiple-personality disorder, you should be pretty much the way you are offline." No matter where you go there you are.

'All things being equal, people do business with and refer business to people they know, like and trust. By this point in the 21st century most of us have gotten past the Madison Avenue slick come-on lines we're constantly fed. I don't know about you, but I'm looking for authenticity, transparency and honesty. Save the slickness. Just tell me the truth. I can make an intelligent buying decision based on truth and appreciation for the consumer. The smart businesses know this and treat their customers with respect.

'On the social side of social networking, when someone sends you a "friend request" on Facebook, you can click on their name and check out their profile before you accept their request. This is probably a smart move. You wouldn't just accept someone's request to connect by mail or phone without knowing who you are connecting with, would you? The same goes for social networking. Only now you can learn about someone far more thoroughly than you could prior to social networking. Whatever you post on your LinkedIn, Facebook or Twitter profile is pretty much public information. You now have the ability to see what someone is posting on their Facebook wall, which groups they are a member of, who their friends are and much more information which gives you some insight into who they are. By extension, this allows you to determine who you are connecting with with far greater accuracy than in the past.

'But no matter how sophisticated you are at social networking, it will never be a replacement for good social skills. And this is huge. Most people figure out what they want to do for a living and forget that unless they are Tom Hanks living on a deserted island with a volleyball named Wilson, people skills are a critical piece of their success puzzle. And herein lies a huge paradox. No matter how many connections you have on social networking platforms, it's all about relationships. You don't have a relationship with your computer and Facebook, you have a relationship "through" your computer and Facebook. So no matter how sophisticated technology gets, we still build true relationships the old-fashioned way. By taking a sincere interest in people.

'The sophisticated person understands that huge doors of opportunity swing on little hinges. When we take a sincere interest in other people, we can build relationships. Real relationships. Not just an "I'm connected to you on Facebook" relationship. You can "connect" with the whole world, but if you don't really "connect", you may as well be looking at a worldwide phonebook.'

● ●

Table 5.1 shows some online dos and don'ts.

Table 5.1: online dos and don'ts

Do	Don't
Be yourself	Connect with those you don't want to
Tell the truth	Use an alter ego
Be a person	Just be a computer
Read people's profiles	
Say thanks	
Leave a 'tip' in the jar—use the 'like' button	

Maintaining your online reputation

Author Hannah Samuel, the 'Reputation Champion', discusses online reputations:

● ●

'American writer Ambrose Bierce is quoted as saying, "Speak when you are angry and you will make the best speech you will ever regret." The explosion of blogs, personalised websites and community and other online interactive forums on the internet has changed the way information is received and processed and how we represent ourselves or find ourselves being represented.

'We are connecting, communicating and revealing personal and professional information about ourselves more openly than ever before. In the time it takes to read this chapter hundreds of hours of video will be uploaded to YouTube.

'We tap out information about ourselves at lightning speed and yet rarely think about the damage that can be caused to our reputation, both online and off, by posting careless remarks and images. Even if we don't write the words ourselves, others are writing about us, and in this digital age of instant upload it's worth remembering that the camera is always rolling, the microphone is always on, and there's no such thing as "off the record".

'It's also worth remembering that the word "cache" means to "conceal" or "hide". How appropriate then that cached pages on the internet bear testament to many a statement or image some would rather forget but that are available to anyone at the click of a link.

'Social media sites and other online forums have enabled consumer communities to develop at incredible speed and give anyone with internet access the opportunity to publish whatever content they choose, largely without being censored. Our electronic footprints can follow us for life, and are available for anyone with access to the internet to view and make judgements about, fairly or otherwise. Find yourself on the wrong end of a blog, or other website posting, and you may find yourself having to defend or refute a reputation you have been given by others. Revenge and malicious attack can be very public indeed on the internet.

'The internet can help others find you, and your products and services if you're in business, quickly and easily. Used well, social media sites can help you engage with a whole new audience of people interested in what you have to say or provide, including potential employers. Be aware, though, that word of mouth has been supplemented by word of mouse, and news travels very far, very fast, on the internet.

'A recent study found 70 per cent of surveyed HR professionals in the US (and 41 per cent in the UK) have rejected a candidate based on online reputation information. However, reputation can also have a positive effect, with 86 per cent of HR professionals in the US, and at least two-thirds of those in the UK and Germany, stating that a positive online reputation influences the candidate's application to some extent. Almost half stated that it influences an application to a great extent.

'Top reasons given for rejecting a candidate include posting of unsuitable photos or videos, concerns about a candidate's lifestyle and inappropriate comments.

'So how can you create a positive online presence on social networking sites while minimising the risks of online reputation damage, now and in the future? Avoiding these sites is an option, but it won't stop people talking about you and you'll be in less of a position to be able to respond should they do so. Instead:

▶ *Choose your site(s) wisely.* Sites themselves have reputations—check them out and decide whether you want to be associated with them. MySpace has fallen in popularity whereas Facebook and LinkedIn have surged.

▶ *Choose your online identity wisely.* As an individual, hiding behind nicknames that could raise eyebrows won't do you any favours. If using the sites for professional purposes, use your own personal or business name, or one close to it. If using sites for personal purposes, make sure you go through every privacy setting and make information available to invited friends only if you don't want the information you post to be seen by anyone connected to the web.

▶ *Choose your online friends and associates wisely.* Quality, rather than quantity, should be the driving force for making and accepting online connections and links. The more friends you're connected with, the more chance there is of being associated with something they say or do that you'd rather not be associated with. Reputation by association is a powerful driver and people will make judgement calls about you based on who you are associated with.

► *Choose your content wisely*. Countless companies and individuals have found out the hard way that once online, photos, videos and comments written in haste can cause significant damage to a reputation. Before uploading anything, ask yourself the question, "Am I happy for this to be associated with me and be viewable by anyone, anywhere, at any time—forever?" If the answer's no—don't post it.

'Millions of people routinely Google companies and individuals every day to see what their online presence is like. What we see and read about people and organisations on the internet massively influences whether we are likely to engage with them ourselves, recommend them to someone we know and trust, or choose to be associated with them, online and off. It's worth thinking about what your online reputation may be saying about you.'

Activity 3

Take a moment and review what has been said about your brand on Google. While it is virtually impossible to do anything about it, you should be aware of both good and bad press.

Playing the name game

Choosing what to call yourself online may seem frivolous and an opportunity to create a form of alter ego but its impact shouldn't be underestimated. What you're known as online can have a major impact on how you are perceived.

Far from being online identities, Twisty Poi, Sex Fruit and Stallion were all blocked by real-life officials when applications were made to register newborns with these names, primarily because it was deemed such names were likely to create 'social hurdles' for the children as they grew up. Nine-year-old Talula Does The Hula From Hawaii (who's actually from New Plymouth) might agree with the officials' stance given that she was so embarrassed by her legal name she petitioned to have it changed.

Intentionally or otherwise, the name we are known by can elicit thoughts and emotions in others that may open doors or slam them shut. Hence the reason most of us think carefully before naming a new arrival Violence or Benson and Hedges (twins) — both genuine name applications! But thinking carefully when choosing a name is something many of us fail to do when we blithely create an identity on social networking sites and internet forums.

The name you choose for your online identities can be instrumental in shaping what people think about you and have long-lasting, possibly negative, effects on your reputation and career. Calling yourself Busta Big Belly, Exam Cheat or Liar-Liar might make you chuckle but is likely to raise doubts and eyebrows among possible employers, professional contacts and others.

In this online era it's important, too, to consider whether having some consistency across the social networking sites you are part of may be important. The ability to link one site with another connects us like never before and will become easier to do in the future. It's worth considering if your LinkedIn, Facebook, Google+ and Twitter profiles are largely consistent and easily recognisable. If one or more of them screams 'avoid at all costs!' or 'got something to hide' to a potential employer or other browser, the chances are your other sites will be 'tainted' accordingly.

Given that a large percentage of companies are using LinkedIn and other social media sites as major sources of information about possible employees and to check out someone's background and expertise, your online identity is more important than ever in terms of creating crucial first, second and third impressions.

Ensuring the name you choose for your online identities works for you rather than against you is relatively straightforward.

Use your real name if you can

Rightly or wrongly, people who use their real name, as opposed to a quirky ID, are generally more highly regarded than those who don't. If your own name's already been taken, consider adding an underscore, or hyphen, to create as close a match to your name as possible. Or, if this proves tricky, using a name that has positive or neutral connotations that can be used in connection with your real name is a good second option—for example, 'KiwiGuy (Chris Merton)'.

Choose the same name for different sites if possible

Whether it's your real name, or an assumed identity, make it easy for browsers to identify you on different sites by using the same or a similar name, if possible. Using the same name on different sites indicates a willingness to be open and traceable on the web, which is generally considered a positive trait.

Secure your name on sites you're not necessarily active on

Even if you don't intend to have an active presence on a particular site, it's worth considering securing the name you want for two reasons:

▶ If you do decide to become active you will have the name you want ready to go.

▶ Securing the name you want will stop others from securing it and posting content that could end up being inadvertently associated with you.

Whether you're in the market for friendship, a lifelong relationship, a new job or simply to share your thoughts and opinions with the world, the name(s) you use online will influence the instant judgements that are made about you and whether others connect, interact and associate with you. Your online name and reputation will only become more important as we all engage in more and more online interaction and information-sharing.

You could, of course, call yourself 'Number 16 Bus Shelter'—another name that was turned down by the registrar of births not too long ago—but you might just find it becomes a road to nowhere.

Make sure you have secured your company and personal usernames on:

▶ Twitter

▶ YouTube

▶ Facebook

▶ Google+

▶ any other site you may use.

Is your social media activity antisocial?

According to Beloit College's 'Mindset' list many young Americans headed to university in 2010 thought Germany has always been one country, Beethoven was a dog rather than a composer and Banana Republic is a fashion store rather than a politically unstable South American dictatorship.

The Gen Xs and Baby Boomers among us may shake our heads at this news, lamenting how 'times change', while Gen Ys may very well feel affronted, and wonder why the alternatives have any relevance at all!

No matter what our age, if we incorrectly assume others have a similar world view to us we may find ourselves faced with blank faces, quizzical looks and wildly different expectations—all of which can have a huge adverse impact on how we are perceived, and this in turn affects our reputation.

Although increasing numbers of us are embracing social media with the intention of having a greater and more immediate connection with our clients and contacts, there is a danger that in doing so we may actually distance ourselves, and disconnect from the very people we want to engage with, particularly if they're not as 'social media savvy' as us.

Hashtags, bitly and RTs (retweets) may be second nature to you. Indeed, you may already have claimed the title 'Mayor of…' (insert favourite cafe name) on foursquare, but if your clients, colleagues and others have no idea what you're talking about, or feel paralysed and unable to respond to your seemingly endless posts and tweets, you're more likely to irritate and annoy, rather than connect and engage.

Unless there is a mutual understanding between you and your contacts regarding jargon and etiquette when using social media sites such as Facebook, Twitter and LinkedIn, rather than creating greater engagement you may, instead, not only confuse, but exclude. If they don't use the sites you use, or feel sidelined or hopeless because they're not even sure how they're supposed to respond, you may earn a reputation for making it harder rather than easier to engage with you, and that's not a good reputation to have.

If you want to win people over rather than alienate them when communicating using social media:

▶ Never assume others are as 'up to speed' as you. Check understanding, and educate and inform as you go in ways that make others feel positive and included rather than social media outcasts.

▶ Make others aware of useful websites and other resources that can help them become more familiar with social media etiquette and jargon and bring them up to speed more quickly.

▶ Avoid using instant messaging chat-speak if the person you're dealing with isn't familiar with it. 'Lol' ('lots of laughs' or 'laugh out loud') isn't funny to someone who doesn't know what it means!

▶ Ensure good old-fashioned phone numbers are clearly visible on your social media profiles, unless, of course, you really do want to alienate people who want to actually speak with you rather than use a keyboard!

▶ Retain your existing website, or create one using your real name as the URL, so it both confirms and becomes a central source of information regarding all your online identity names and their web addresses.

▶ Continue to use traditional communication methods such as texting or plain-old phone calls alongside your social media activity until the person you're communicating with lets you know they're happy to connect using the same sites as you.

Remember, a lack of response or interaction may simply be due to the fact that they don't understand your message or know how to respond. Some may be put off by the apparent casualness of the communication and may not want to respond in the same media or format. Others simply may not have immediate access to technology that would enable them to respond. Never assume everyone's as instantly connected as you.

Perception is reality. If the people you're trying to engage with feel excluded or intimidated by your use of social media, then it would be wise to go out of your way to make it easy for them to communicate with you using traditional communication tools until they feel more comfortable retweeting right back @ya!

Minimising reputational risks online

If you or your organisation finds itself the subject of internet comment or footage you'd rather wasn't there, taking action is essential.

Patrick Doyle, president of Domino's Pizza, was right to act swiftly and respond to a video on YouTube showing an employee putting cheese up his nose before adding it to a pizza waiting to be cooked, and then sneezing all over it. This wasn't an isolated incident. Similar video clips are uploaded online daily by employees and others who probably don't think about the reputational damage and consequences. For those who do, it may be the ultimate act of revenge. Given the ease with which anyone can record someone, or something, and upload it to the internet, it will certainly continue to happen.

The Domino's video went viral and was viewed by hundreds of thousands of people online in a matter of days, and was picked up by major media worldwide. For any business it would be a reputation nightmare. For a global franchise business with a 50-year history it was potentially disastrous.

Understanding that similar acts might affect your organisation at some point is the first step in developing a plan to minimise it happening.

Do:

▶ *set clear expectations and guidelines*. Ensure staff are aware of what's acceptable and permitted, and what's not, on an ongoing basis. Ensure they are aware of possible consequences of inappropriate behaviour.

▶ *encourage a culture of trust and respect*. Inappropriate behaviour often occurs when others 'egg them on'. Reduce the likelihood of this happening by making people feel valued, and valuable, in ways that are meaningful to them.

▶ *identify areas of concern and address them openly*. If food preparation takes place out of sight, for example, bring it into the open so customers can see their meal being prepared in front of them—something Subway has done very successfully.

Don't:

▶ *think 'it'll never happen to us'*. It's entirely possible that it will! Identify 'what if?' scenarios and work out how these could be avoided before having to deal with them in real life.

▶ *threaten, intimidate or bully staff*. It may make them more determined to undermine you and damage your brand, especially if they've already made the decision to move on anyway.

▶ *assume the people who work for you care as much about your business as you do*. Some staff may act vengefully, others may simply not think about the consequences of their actions. Either way, once online, information can travel very far, very fast.

Whether an online video clip or image is real or a hoax, deliberate or inadvertent, doesn't matter. True or not, once it's online, it can be there forever, damaging your personal and professional reputation irreparably. Philosopher Joseph Hall was wise when he said, around 200 years ago, 'A reputation, once broken, may possibly be repaired, but the world will always keep its eyes on the spot where the crack was.'

Conclusion of chapter 5

If you are well known for supplying great information, it will go a long way to establishing your great online reputation, so it's important to keep up the content part of your plan. Use a good proportion of your own material, but no more than, say, around 30 per cent: you don't want to be seen as a spammer.

Remember to be yourself online and then you won't forget your online manners either.

CHAPTER 6
YouTube explained

Key areas we will cover in chapter 6:

✓ why create a video?

✓ some real examples

✓ quick video ideas

✓ creating your video

✓ uploading your video.

Video marketing is fast becoming a popular way to explain a product or service, and sites such as YouTube are very popular. Think of YouTube as a resource channel to find the answer to your question, as well as an entertainment centre for funny videos.

Quick stats www.youtube.com

Here are some interesting YouTube stats:

▶ it was founded in 2005

▶ one billion users visit each month

▶ six billion hours are watched each month

▶ 70 per cent of traffic is from outside the USA

▶ 40 per cent of time watched is on mobile.

Why create a video in the first place?

It's that exposure word again. How great would it be if one of your videos had millions of views worldwide and everyone was talking about your brand? And all for the cost of making a great video?

But in order for a video to go viral and be shared across the world, you need to really home in on emotion. Your video needs to be either very funny, sad, loving or any other emotion you want to use, but the key is emotion: pull on the viewers' heartstrings or laughter strings.

We've all received emails in our inbox with links to funny videos, from funny home movies and footage of cats, to funny commercials and professional training videos. The common denominator is that they are all funny.

When you see a funny video, you are more likely to pass it on to your friends or simply post it to your Facebook wall for all to see. Imagine if you are Heineken, and your series of funny commercials is being passed around from one person's network to another: the exposure you get from that could be massive, and the only cost is the cost of the video. If you aim that video content at your target market at the same time, it's hard to lose. The trick is to make something good enough that people want to share.

As our lives get busier our attention span starts to wane a little, so a short sharp video explaining something you need to understand is another great way of accessing that information. I no longer use the 'help' function in Word or Excel: if I want to learn how to put a column into a spreadsheet, for example, I simply go to YouTube, type in the search terms I need, and pick a quick video to show me how to do it. It really suits my style of learning, as it does many others too: if I can see how something is done, rather than read about it, it is much clearer and quicker for me to understand.

It would be great if your videos went viral and achieved massive exposure but in reality very few do. But you do need to aim for your video to be passed around, and even if you don't get to the millions of views, the more people who see what you have created the more people who are aware of your product or service.

What are people watching

Over the last 12 months there has been a definite shift in which videos get the really big viewer numbers. It's no longer the lost dog that gets found, or the silly antics a cat gets up to when its owner isn't looking, but the music videos. We have had music videos for many years now, but they really do seem to have taken off for the top artist names. Indeed, as of writing this, the top 10 videos by views includes Miley Cyrus's *Wrecking Ball*, Lady Gaga, Shakira, PSY, LMFAO, Eminem and JLo, with Justin Bieber being the first on the list to break a billion. But it's *Gangnam Style* from PSY that takes the top spot with nearly two billion views. The only one in the top 10 that is not an artist sits at number 4, and is the original 'Charlie bit my finger' with a very healthy 670 million views.

Rather than the mass videos we have seen in the past, I think that now there are stars that stand out within our interest group or niche. For example, if you are really interested in cycling, there will be a hot video doing the rounds in the cycling genre, or perhaps a how-to video within the home-baking genre. The exception here might be the Super Bowl ads that are created each year.

Real example: Super Bowl

Every year, ad agencies are tasked with creating the commercial that everyone will be talking about from the Super Bowl. It's the Oscars equivalent for commercials, with great analysis about what has worked and why, and what has not. Indeed mashable. com publishes the best of the Super Bowl ads and how they are trending pretty much as they happen. The mainly 30-second spots are probably the most expensive in the world because of the many millions of viewers watching the match and watching this year's ad creations. We are even starting to see ad teasers that the big brands are using to test the water, trying to gauge the viewers' reaction before the launch of the full-size ad on the big day, and hoping it will be the big one. This is quite a clever way to start people talking about your brand, and if you have the budget to do so, make adjustments to the longer version or scrap it all together and start afresh. Big money is at stake to get it absolutely right during such a popular sporting highlight of the year.

Real example: Blendtec

Back in 2010, a regular household name in food blenders, Blendtec, was looking for something a little more innovative to catch its audience's eye and gain that valuable exposure at the same time. Why not see what the blender can successfully blend? A whole series of videos was created over a period of time demonstrating different items being blended, with the most popular item being the iPhone. With a video channel creating over 240 million views of the 'mad professor', who was in fact the founder of Blendtec, Tom Dickson, blending items such as the iPhone to dust, it quickly skyrocketed the Blendtec name and sales. The series of 'will it blend' videos blends all kinds of things such as boxes of matches, a camcorder, Bic lighters and the iPhone5. The series is so popular you can buy T-shirts with the slogan 'Tom Dickson is my homeboy' on it. After many more different blending attempts, the videos still go on today, probably making the Blendtec channel one of the oldest running and most successful.

What about the smaller companies like me?

Frog Recruitment has used video to fill positions that are a bit out of the norm with great success. Take a look at 'MOTAT career video', which was produced to show what goes on in the transport museum on a daily basis and to introduce the rest of the team to the potential new employee. A low-cost way to create a bit of a buzz, fill a position and promote a great cause at the same time. Maybe you could use this approach to fill an exciting or unique position at your company?

John Spence, author and business-improvement expert, regularly uses video to review business books: a great way to show his expertise as a business writer, gain more valuable exposure to his own personal brand and add value to the tribe that follows him in the business world. If John says a book is good, it usually is. I regularly visit his site to watch his short informative videos. What could you review to gain that sort of exposure?

Tony Vidler, an advisor to the financial advice industry, has created a whole series of Top Tips, very short and succinct video tips aimed at financial advisors to help them grow their own businesses. They tend to be around a minute long and are top and tailed with his logo and contact details, great for when someone shares one. He releases them at regular intervals to keep his brand on people's radars, and adding some value at the same time.

Corning Glass created a couple of very popular videos about how glass will feature in our future. It's a very technical product, but the videos are presented as a cross between looking to the future and what we can already see happening now with things such as glass mobile phones and cooktops.

Video ideas

Some simple ideas for your video:

- welcome message on your website

- demonstration of your product

- your current TV adverts

- insider's view of your business

- industry tips

- client testimonials

- event footage with testimonials

- project unfolding to completion

- holiday wishes.

Making your video

Many people's first thoughts about making a video are: what will it cost, what equipment will I need and what should I do in the video in the first place?

The first part of the question is easy enough to answer as the cost of creating a video can run from a handful of dollars to many thousands, so it really depends on your budget and what you are trying to achieve. With video tools now so readily available, even if you don't own a video camera yourself, you may know someone you can borrow one from.

Some benefits of using video:

▶ You can explain a technical product easily.

▶ You can add personality to your product.

▶ Viewers can meet the team.

▶ It has the ability to be passed around for greater exposure.

▶ It's relatively cheap.

The content of the video is a little more complicated and I will give you some more ideas of what others are doing later on.

Your equipment is important, but it doesn't need to be film-industry high-definition standard that costs the earth: you can now get some very good small cameras that will do the job perfectly well. I personally use an HD Flip camera that has built-in audio on both sides and cost me a couple of hundred dollars, but iPhones do a decent job too and there are many more on the market. I would look out for one that will allow you to use a microphone with it, because you may be forgiven for bad lighting, but never for bad audio. If no-one can hear you, they won't stick around to watch the rest of your video.

With regard to the lighting, natural is always best, with the light shining on your face rather than on the back of your head if you are presenting, but do a dummy run first to check if you need to make any adjustments.

Most cameras will record for a couple of hours on a full battery, which is ample to get the shots you need, but you will need to then edit your video, which is not as hard as you might think. If you use a PC or laptop, you more than likely have Windows Movie Maker already installed, and if you are on a Mac, you will have iMovie. The first time I put a short movie together it took me a couple of hours to figure it out, but the second one was finished in just a few minutes and I used the resource of YouTube to do it. I simply put into the search box what I was looking to do with Movie Maker such as add music, and watched the video. You can even add in a branded first slide and credits at the end if you so wish. Don't forget to add your company details so people can get hold of you.

> **Activity 1**
>
> Start practising with your video editing software on your computer to see how easy it is! Find a video on YouTube to show you how to use your software if you are unsure.

Following are some things you should think about when making your video.

Length

The optimum length of a video has dropped to around 90 seconds, which is surprisingly ample time for you to get your message across. The first five seconds of any video is the most important part and you will really need to grab the viewers' attention in this time if you want them to watch the rest of your video. Dive straight in, otherwise you will find people switching off in droves, as we just don't have the time available that we used to have.

If you are making a series such as a short TV show that you are planning to do regularly, about eight minutes is your maximum. Unless you are interviewing a really special person, videos of 30+ minutes are long gone, so bear this in mind when you plan your video. For a video interview, stick to around 15 minutes.

Content

Think about what you want to achieve in the first place. Is it to create a short series of value-added videos to share with your clients and prospects, or is it more about brand exposure, creating a funny video that you hope will get noticed and go viral? Of course there is no point making a video that is not going to be passed on, so even if it is an educational video, make it so content-rich that others will find it beneficial and want to pass it on.

Air New Zealand has made a series of light-hearted safety videos for its flight attendants to work with as it has realised that by keeping them relevant, amusing and updated, more travellers will pay attention and watch the serious message they contain. They can all be seen on YouTube; many have amassed millions of views.

Interviews are an easy way to add flavour to your site so consider who you could ask in your industry that would be willing to share their expertise with you. Think about industry experts, famous people you are connected to in some way, people of interest in general, or the lighter side of your company's management team, but make it interesting and content-rich.

Dos and don'ts

A few important dos:

- ▶ Use a microphone.
- ▶ Consider your lighting (not too light or dark).
- ▶ Reduce background noise.
- ▶ Decide on a content plan for a series of videos.
- ▶ Create video regularly, whether that be monthly or quarterly.

A few important don'ts:

- ▶ Never upload video you do not have the rights for, such as concert footage.
- ▶ Never add distasteful content. Read the terms and conditions if you are unsure.
- ▶ Don't infringe copyright.
- ▶ Don't leave abusive comments.
- ▶ Don't make it too long—viewers will turn it off.

Activity 2

Brainstorm what content you could put into a series of videos.

Setting up your YouTube channel and uploading your video

Once you have shot and edited your video and you are happy with it, the obvious place to post it is www.youtube.com, so set yourself up an account or 'channel'. Your account name should be your business name if it is not already taken, and there is space to fill out a bit more information on the profile page, so make use of it.

You can customise your channel look with images by clicking on the 'customise channel' link in settings, and while you are in there, click on 'activity sharing' and fill out your Twitter and Facebook details and what you would like to share. This is another easy step to utilise so that when you upload a new video, mark a video as a favourite, or 'like' a video it will automatically update your network for you.

Activity 3

Set up your YouTube channel and customise the page with your brand colours.

Uploading

To upload a new video, simply click on 'upload' and follow the simple instructions. Your video can be in a range of formats, be up to 20 GB in size, and be in high definition. If your video is longer than 15 minutes, you will have to use the 'increase my limit' link at the bottom of the page to be able to do so. Uploading the video takes a few minutes to process, so you can fill out the rest of the information while you are waiting.

It will ask you for:

▶ *A title*. This needs to accurately reflect what the video is about but it also needs to contain keywords. I usually add the title followed by my name or company name, depending on the available space.

▶ *Description*. What is the video about? Get those keywords in there too. You want your video to be found easily by others typing in relevant search criteria.

▶ *Tags*. Tags are simply the main keywords about your video's content. This is how people will find your video so it is important they are accurate.

▶ *Category and privacy*. These are self-explanatory, you just need to choose what options best suit your needs. If you want everyone to be able to see your video, select the public setting. You can keep a video private if you are not quite happy with it and want to edit it later.

When your video is uploaded fully you can begin promoting it. There are plenty of places to promote your video or video channel and here are a few ideas for you:

▶ vimeo.com

▶ viddler.com

▶ screen.yahoo.com

▶ tubemogul.com

▶ blinkx.com

▶ your blog

▶ your Facebook page (as an upload rather than a link)

▶ your website

▶ your LinkedIn profile

▶ your email signature (linked to your channel)

▶ your newsletter.

You can get the code to embed your video into most of these sites direct from your YouTube channel page. It is just a case of copying and pasting into the right place.

Where else can I post it?

Once your video is live on YouTube, you can:

▶ tweet the link via Twitter

▶ add it to your Facebook page either as a link or as an upload

▶ upload it to your rich media section on LinkedIn

▶ set up a Slideshare account and upload it there too

▶ upload the link as a discussion point on LinkedIn if it warrants it.

You can repeat any or all of these after a month.

Promoting your video

YouTube is now owned by Google, so you can promote your video just like you can with **Google AdWords**, and you can see examples of this all over the YouTube site. Companies both large and small can make use of it depending on their budget and you will very often see some of the big brands promoting their video along the top space of your screen.

Subscribing to others

By clicking the 'subscribe' button on someone else's channel, you will be notified when they have uploaded another video, but you will also find that if you subscribe to theirs, they may well return the favour and subscribe back. That means they are notified when you upload another video, so you are creating another set of connections to communicate with.

Social media success story: Frog Recruitment

Frog Recruitment is a forward-thinking recruitment company that uses many of the social media channels to showcase its brand, and add value for its clients and prospects.

Frog started using video several years ago and has revelled in the benefits of the cut-through it provides. This is where the action is happening as our consumption of video grows and grows. As Jane Kennelly says:

'When Frog Recruitment launched in 2002 it was with several pithy objectives in mind. One of these, unashamedly, was to change the rules of the game with recruitment. Frog identified that the main area that needed impact was in the provision of an improved service for candidates by creating an experience for them and communicating with them. For clients, it was about educating, informing and clearly demonstrating the link between employer branding and the candidate by leading the way with new practices.

'It was very much in keeping with our company philosophy that we gravitated towards social media channels early on, and we were determined to embrace them. This was a time when the market was very tight and our attendances at international conferences confirmed that social media trends from the US were becoming well established in the recruitment industry. Terms like cyber sleuth, gamification, video position descriptions, microblogging, microsites and social networking were being thrown about and to us, so it was as plain as the nose on your face that we needed to get in, get started and make it authentic and accessible for all.

'We now know that the development of social media channels is the biggest thing to hit the recruitment industry since the invention of the telephone. And it is all about experimentation.

(continued)

Social media success story: Frog Recruitment *(cont'd)*

'Knowing the impact was going to be intense, we decided to evolve a role within the business several years ago: Communications/ Social Media. The focus here was to embrace and drive our connections with clients and candidates alike, through the development of integrated channels. This is one place where experimentation and testing new directions is A-OK!

Platforms

'From a platform perspective, we decided to focus our energies on LinkedIn, Twitter and Facebook. We write blogs, create video content, communicate to segmented groups and share information on a weekly basis. And we have learned some interesting things...

- Facebook is a very good option for targeted advertising. Not many people wanted to be our "friend"; as to be friends with a recruiter on Facebook could be considered a bit too obvious! Advertising on Facebook, on the other hand, is a good idea, particularly if you wish to connect with a specific target demographic/geographic region. For example, in one campaign we were able to serve an advertisement up to 2400 product managers in NZ and received 14 applications as a result and the position was successfully filled. To beef up our Facebook power we developed a tab within the architecture of Facebook to allow browsers to view the roles we are advertising.

- Twitter: a positive surprise. We underestimated the impact this might have and have enjoyed building our community here. From automatic live updates to a dedicated hashtag called #FrogTalent, our Twitter activity has increased interaction, applications and visitors to the company site.

- LinkedIn: the recruiter's and careerseeker's dream. Early in the piece we engaged the services of a trainer [the author of this very book!] to make sure we were seeing the full capacity LinkedIn has to offer as a business tool. And it has a lot to offer. The uptake has been so strong with the benefits of using LinkedIn becoming more and more apparent. Once you have completed your profile, joined a few groups, chatted to a few people and connected with others, you can soon see the power of this networking machine.

- Integration is the key to success here. These platforms are not successful on their own, so we have developed ways to integrate our advertising, content and growth across these three channels, and are constantly looking for new ways to expand our reach. Everything from our website to e-communications, social networks, advertising and marketing is linked to drive business from one platform to the other, so our customers can communicate and engage with us in multiple ways to suit their requirements. As a result we have seen our website visitation rates jump and have seen similar results from our e-communication and social network audience.

'As we are undergoing massive change in our industry, the talent acquisition landscape has moved from "the war for talent" to "candidate engagement and experience" —even more reason to be confident in the social media environment.

New skills

'As we have grappled with the impact of the changing scene, we have asked ourselves: "What skills will be required by those involved in the recruitment function of tomorrow, in order to be ahead of the game?"

In researching the DNA a recruiter needs for the future, the following vital attributes have emerged:

- *Savvy operators.* Every person in the organisation needs to be more than just an operator. They have to be curious, technically competent, investigative and creative, so they can use these tools proactively.

(continued)

Social media success story: Frog Recruitment *(cont'd)*

- *Social media expertise*. Essentially this is about creating competitive advantage. This allows the market to be navigated for opportunities and for talent. It allows a variety of conversations to occur in an authentic way. Supported by analytics the reporting provides insight into effectiveness—in real time!

- *Connecting confidence*. It's out with transactional activity and in with relationship development. Opportunities pop up for those who take the time to create a social network. And it's never been easier.

Time and content

'One of the factors that did perplex us in the early days was exactly how much time should be allocated to social media work and where on earth do the content ideas stem from?

'Due to the patterns that emerged, we decided the time question should be changed to: "What is the minimum time you should spend?" We believe you need to be adding content at least once a week to keep content fresh and your audience engaged.

As to content? Well, along with great writing skills, one needs to be a good reader. Being widely read across a range of books and publications sparks ideas for content. And after a while you begin to realise that it's not a fully researched novel that is needed, but ideas or thoughts or stories, explored one at a time in a succinct way to make them easy to read and digest.

The future

'Some thoughts about the future of recruitment and social media:

- From our perspective integrated platforms rule. Leveraging the information posted is sensible and time-efficient.

- We are being challenged to communicate in a vastly different way. Not all people want or desire to be social media aficionados but once they are engaged, they are hooked.

- Be prepared for things to go mobile—for example, interviews, assessments and training are going mobile and we need to communicate with people on the move. Frog launched a mobile optimised career portal in 2013 and since then application numbers via mobile are up to 24 per cent.

- Be prepared for the virtual world, for example, work, play, relationships, learning. The virtual employee is becoming ever more popular and acceptable.

- Roles, work and learning will all become personalised, just as advertising, marketing and communication trends have shown in recent years.

- Crowd-sourcing, tagging and networks are being used to find people. Retaining and engaging talent will be developed through learning, networks, communities and intangibles. People will become deeply connected to their organisations and you can guarantee lower turnover if people feel connected and a part of it.

- Shrinking organisations will move towards more outsourcing and contingency work. We are already experiencing this trend with our clients who have partnered with us or seconded our staff to work within their organisations on large, customised recruiting projects.'

Quick tip

Don't just stop at one video; try to create a regular series, even if it's only twice per year.

Conclusion of chapter 6

Video really does give your business another tool to make use of in many different ways, and once you have made a couple successfully, you will no doubt get the bug to make more and more. You could be pleasantly surprised how your customers and prospects receive your great new videos.

Check back to your content plan from the beginning and see how you thought video could be a part of it. Hopefully you now have some very clear ideas how you can use it creatively.

CHAPTER 7
Google+ and why it's important for SEO

Key areas we will cover in chapter 7:

✓ using Google+ for SEO

✓ why Google+ is different from the rest

✓ the power of Google authorship.

Google+ is a social media platform that sits somewhere between Facebook and LinkedIn. Owned by Google, it has great search engine capabilities, particularly for a bricks-and-mortar business.

Quick stats plus.google.com

Here are some interesting Google+ stats:

▶ it was launched in 2011

▶ there are over a billion registered users worldwide

▶ it recently stipulated that if you wanted any other Google product such as Gmail, you had to open a Google+ account too, which is one reason it has created such a large user base, but not all users are active.

Advantages of Google+

With Facebook being your coffee shop of conversation, and LinkedIn being your boardroom, it's hard to see where Google+ fits in, and that has meant its growth and active user base has been slow to catch on.

It's just like when a new bar opens up in your town—until your mates start hanging out there, you stick with the usual existing haunts, and it's exactly the same in the online space. If your buddies are happily using Facebook, you will too—there is little point in going to a place where there is little action from your friends and acquaintances; it's a bit lonely and so no-one bothers.

However, there are some definite advantages to having a Google+ page, and Google has thought very hard about how it can bring some unique functionality to the platform.

The first one is very definitely the **search engine optimisation** (SEO) aspect. Obviously Google owns the Google+ accounts, just as it owns YouTube, so when it comes to popping up high on search results, it's going to favour its own content from its own members over and above another platform or website. Having a Google+ account definitely influences the results, which is why more and more people are starting to take it seriously.

The second key difference is the ability to hold a Google+ **Hangout**, which is basically a live video chat similar to Skype. Several people can get together and enjoy an intimate but virtual conversation: as of writing this, it's a maximum of 10 users. Anyone with an account can organise one and send an invitation to their circles. Imagine if Richard Branson or Bruno Mars decided to do an impromptu Hangout and you were one of the first 10 to get the notification and click attend—how cool would that be? Others have done it. Great quality and easy to use and a great way to demonstrate your product or offer help to a group of people free of charge.

The third thing that Google+ has is the ability to send an email to another Google user without actually knowing their email address. You won't actually be privy to seeing their email address but your message will land in their inbox as long as they haven't disabled their email notifications. There is an issue in that if they reply back to you by hitting reply, it goes to a no-reply address and so it may cause confusion or upset, so be aware, but this is mentioned at the bottom of the email from Google so it shouldn't cause too many problems.

Fourthly, you can put those that you follow into circles. Think of a circle as a folder. Yes, you can make lists or folders on Facebook so that you only post to certain people rather than post publicly all the time, but circles on Google+ go one step further. When you post an update, the public selection will come up, but then you have the option to send the post to certain circles, meaning they will then receive the update as an email too if you have opted for that option. As I have already mentioned, this can be turned off, but I wonder how many have done so? Think of circles simply as groups of people such as friends, acquaintances, heroes, business connections etc. and name them accordingly. There is no limit to the number of circles you can have.

The rest of the functionality of Google+ is pretty much the same as Facebook and LinkedIn, with the ability to:

▶ post content

▶ share content

▶ comment on content

▶ like (+1)

▶ send messages

▶ create events

▶ include links

▶ add video

▶ add photos

▶ use hashtags

▶ @replies

▶ build a following (circles).

Who should have a Google+ page

So who should be using a Google+ page? Is it for every business? I would say the answer to that is a resounding yes, if only for the SEO benefits. It's also a really important tool for a business that might not otherwise even bother with a website, such as a local fish and chip shop or corner grocery store. Think about how you yourself use the search function of Google. If you were new to the area, maybe even visiting on holiday, you would probably put 'fish and chips' and the town you are in into the search box and hit enter from your smartphone. If there is a Google+ page or even a Google Places page (more on Places pages in chapter 10), it will come up in the listing along with a map to where the location is. There might also be the opening hours, telephone number and the physical address details, so all in all very handy and convenient. The fact that the service is all free is a great incentive for any business no matter how small to get started and gain some online presence. Add into that the customer reviews that the local fish and chip shop could get from visitors to the page, it's a no-brainer.

Real example: Chamberlains Quality Fish and Chips

There is a fish and chip shop in the UK called Chamberlains Quality Fish and Chips. They have a brief Google+ page (it's obvious they don't use it because it never gets updated) and while it only has a handful of followers, it has had over 45 000 views with 19 people leaving positive reviews about the food. Now with those numbers of people visiting their page, they should really take advantage and make the effort to update it with menu changes, special offers, great images and customer comments.

Creating a Google+ page

It's easy enough to get started: simply go to www.accounts.google. com and create a Google account if you don't already have one, then follow the steps to creating a Google+ page.

> **Activity 1**
>
> Set up your Google+ page and copy some of the content from your Facebook page across so it doesn't look empty. It has now become part of your digital marketing strategy and needs updating regularly.

You can and should have more than one admin or page manager and Google actually allows you to have up to 50 at any one time. Only the page owner can add or remove page managers, although a page manager can remove themselves.

Adding a manager

To add another manager to your Google+ page, simply click settings and look for managers. Click *Add manager* then you can either enter their email address or invite them by their profile, so then you just need to click *Invite*.

This page then displays all of the active managers, as well as anyone you have just invited to become a manager. When the manager invitation has been accepted, the owner of the Google+ page will be notified via email. It's worth pointing out that the page owner and all of the managers can view the names and email addresses of the other managers listed on this page.

Removing a manager

To remove a manager, or to remove yourself as a manager of a page, simply click the **X** associated with the person you'd like to remove.

When a manager is removed, both the former manager and the page owner will be notified and advised who removed them. This is a great bit of security, particularly if you have a large team looking after the page.

Transferring ownership of a page

If you are unsure about who the page owner should be, whether it is the business owner or the marketing department, for instance, or if someone leaves the company, you can always transfer ownership if necessary later on. The person you transfer ownership to must have been an existing manager of the page for at least two weeks. If you don't have any managers, you need to first invite the person to become a manager and then wait for them to accept their invitation. When an owner transfers ownership to someone else, the old owner automatically becomes a manager of the page and the transfer of ownership happens immediately—no confirmation is necessary from the new owner. It's worth noting that switching ownership of the page does not switch the ownership of other Google services linked to your page. Just make sure you are using Google+ as the relevant page before you add or remove anyone.

The internal pages

Let's look at the basic page functionality. Like the other platforms, Google changes things and adds things with the wind, but the basics will usually stay the same.

Home page

This is where you will see all of the news that those that you follow or have in circles have posted, and you can comment and share and so on from here.

Profile page

This is the place where you can see all of your own posts and share your content with those in your circles. From a search point of view, the more people that have you in their circles the better because Google knows you are real and not spam, and also because if so many people are interested in what you have to say, it figures you are an authority.

People page

This is where you can find people to put in circles and see who has you in circles too.

Communities page

There is a whole array of various communities you might want to join, so see what interests you and dive into a conversation. Communities are a great way to share and contribute to a common interest group and meet some new people at the same time: they are great for online networking. From foodies to football, book clubs to inspiration, there is something for all by way of photo sharing, one to one (or more) in a Hangout, or taking part in events, and just like Facebook, you can invite your Google+ buddies to the group.

Other functionality

There are a couple of other areas that you will see on other platforms, and they are hashtags and events.

Hashtags

When you post something on your page, hashtags will automatically be included for you, which saves you time thinking about what they might be—if you are like me, I forget most times anyway! You can then either change them or add more in.

Events

From your home page, you can create and share events just like you can on Facebook. You can add an image, choose whether to allow your friends to invite others or not, and decide exactly who you want to invite rather than just posting it publicly on your page. Fill in the rest of the event details such as time, date and location and you are all set to go.

Additionally, by going to the events tab set with the rest of the main navigation, you can also check on other events that are going on throughout Google+, not just the ones you may have been invited to or have organised.

Great examples

There are many examples of brands using Google+ well, so take a look at some of these to get some inspiration about how you can use it for your business:

- plus.google.com/+starbucks

- plus.google.com/+wholefoods

- plus.google.com/+Nordstrom

- plus.google.com/+marksandspencer

- plus.google.com/+benandjerrys

Videos

As Google also owns YouTube, video integration is very easy. If you want to post a video, you have the option of either uploading it to your page, finding other people's video on YouTube and linking to it, or searching through your own video content list on YouTube. You can even record video from the video link.

Google authorship

If you write regularly on your blog or posts for another site, you can now marry up that great content with your Google+ profile so that Google knows it's come from you and can attribute it accordingly. That means that when you write a post and put a byline of 'Author Linda Coles', for example, as long as your Google+ profile page is in the same name, it will see it's you. What that means is when someone is searching on Google for you, not only will your articles and posts show up, but it will automatically post your profile picture next to the article, creating a better and more appealing visual for the person searching. You will need to go to https://plus.google.com/authorship and follow the easy steps to set it up. You only need to do this once. Be aware it can take a while for Google to recognise your great posts and authorship, but it's definitely worth doing.

Even if you don't have the time to fill your Google+ page with great content just yet, create your page, link it to your blog or website and set the unique page URL to grab your name before someone else takes it. Make sure you are happy with your URL before you accept it as it can't be changed later. If you think it will be a while before you can afford to spend any time on it, why not use the header image as a sign to say you are under construction and use an image of a concrete truck for a bit of fun?

Conclusion of chapter 7

Consider how Google+ can work for you. If you are a bricks-and-mortar business, you need a Google+ page as people will be searching for you via Google to find your location and opening hours. Even if you can't commit to updating your page every day, commit to checking it regularly and uploading some fresh content when you can because when a visitor finds you, you want to give the right impression and encourage them to make contact.

Pinterest and pinning the best images

Key areas we will cover in chapter 8:

✓ why great images matter

✓ using Pinterest for content elsewhere.

Scrapbooking has long been the hobby of many and so it makes sense there is an electronic version of the popular pastime for the 21st century—it's called Pinterest.

Quick stats www.pinterest.com

Here are some interesting Pinterest stats:

▶ it was launched in 2010

▶ it has approximately 50 million users

▶ pinners are mainly female

▶ it's online scrapbooking

▶ it can be linked to Facebook, Twitter and Google+

▶ there are mobile versions available.

Online scrapbooking made simple

The beauty of the digital version of scrapbooking is that everyone can see your scrapbooks if you have your privacy settings set so, allowing you to share your favourite things for all to see. If you are a bricks-and-mortar store that sells products, this is another great option to utilise to gain more sets of eyeballs looking at what you have to offer, particularly if you have a dreamy product such as food, design or fashion.

The secret to Pinterest success is sharing beautiful images for others—and yourself—to admire and dream about. Imagine being able to gaze at perfect images of food, travel destinations, wedding dresses, fast cars, fashion and more—whatever your interests.

In fact, any product that produces beautiful images and allows someone to dream will work on Pinterest. You can become a curator of your niche or product, drive traffic back to your main website, find like-minded people with your content and develop your own online profile within your field on Pinterest.

What is a pin?

Every image that you post to your Pinterest page, either directly from your computer or one that you found on another website, is a pin. When someone likes what you have posted they pass it on by reposting or repinning it. You pin images onto **boards** instead of into a physical scrapbook and that's about it for the jargon side of Pinterest.

You don't have to spend a fortune buying images, though. You can instantly pin images from other websites as you see them. This can be done either by clicking on a Pin It button downloaded to your browser bar, or by clicking the Pin It buttons that show alongside an image. You now commonly see the Facebook Like button doing a similar job. These little sharing calls to action are much more commonplace today than ever before, so the more you have on your own main website to encourage others to share your product images, the better it is for you.

Setting up your Pinterest page

Let's have a look at the mechanics of setting up your own Pinterest profile and boards.

Create your profile

You can create either a personal or a business page, depending on what you want from your page. I have created a combination personal and business page because I am Blue Banana, so it makes sense for me to drive traffic to one place rather than two. My page is called 'Blue Banana 20—Linda Coles' so anyone looking for either name will find it.

Fill out the basic info in the boxes as you go, making sure to add in your website as well as links to your other social channels. The more you can cross-share your content the better, and it's more time efficient. Add your profile picture and that's about it.

Activity 1

Set up your Pinterest page. Find interesting boards from others that you admire and follow them, both for learning and finding great content to share.

Create some boards

Think outside the box for your board names: get creative as well as obvious. For instance, you might split your travel boards into 'places I have been' and 'places I want to visit' and 'places I would like to get married' and so on, thereby creating three very different boards on a similar subject.

If you are in the B2B sector like me, it can be tricky to come up with board names for your industry that contain great images, so I have created some called 'cool blue things' (obviously because of Blue Banana), 'I aspire to meet...' and 'inspirational quotes' as well as boards on social media and building relationships. Pinterest is certainly more relevant to some industries than others; here are a few really good examples of great boards:

- ▶ www.pinterest.com/wholefoods
- ▶ www.pinterest.com/gap
- ▶ www.pinterest.com/gucci
- ▶ www.pinterest.com/nordstrom
- ▶ www.pinterest.com/pretzelcrisps

They all have great photos and are all very dream-worthy, just what Pinterest is about, and there are also some quite quirky board ideas. I particularly like Pretzel Crisps Genius Hacks board www.pinterest.com/pretzelcrisps/genius-hacks/ because it is really helpful information for around the home.

Think about some of the boards you would like to keep for yourself, nothing to do with your business, but a place to store your dreams and aspirations, your secret plans and your bright ideas. They don't all have to be public boards, you can make private ones too, as well as public ones that you can share with a nominated someone else. For instance, in developing my last book cover, I pinned some ideas to a board named 'book cover ideas' and shared it with my publisher so she could see my thoughts and add her own in too, making it a collaboration while at the same time allowing everyone else to see them. With secret boards, you can invite certain others to view them, which is really useful if you are planning your wedding and you don't want the groom to see what you are planning but you do want your future sister-in-law to be able to see and perhaps contribute.

Whatever you name your boards, make the headings short and relevant, including a keyword if possible. You want the whole board name to show rather than ending in '...', so use no more than 20 characters including spaces.

You can also rearrange your boards in order so that when visitors land on your Pinterest page for the first time, your best or most relevant boards show up top. Likewise, the main image on each board can be changed to the best one, with the others displaying along the bottom. First impressions matter.

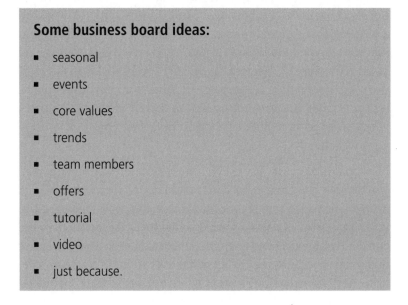

Some business board ideas:

- seasonal
- events
- core values
- trends
- team members
- offers
- tutorial
- video
- just because.

Pinning

You can find content to share from the search function or from the drop-down menu on your profile page. You will find pictures on just about everything possible apart from pornography, which is a definite no-no. Anything from animals to women's fashion, there is even a popular section to see what is hot right now. Some of these images have been pinned thousands of times: imagine if you were the generator of that image, perhaps from your own website — that's great exposure for you.

While I am writing this I am skipping between Pinterest and writing and I have just re-pinned a delicious-looking lemon, Greek yoghurt and cream cheese cake that has caught my eye. The nice thing about it is that the whole recipe on how to make the cake is attached as well as the **pin** creator and comments from others. Once I have pinned it, another option pops up and that is to embed the whole image and recipe onto my own website, linking back again to the originator. Now if I was in the food business, I might do it, but it's not going to work on a website about digital marketing. Shame! If on the other hand you were in the food business, you could create a whole page on your main website devoted to dreamy food pins to make your own site even more appealing, or turn your favourite board into a banner image running across a web page that updates when you add new pins, all by adding a short piece of code to your website.

But you don't have to just re-pin from boards already on Pinterest: you can pin great images as you find them on other websites. The ultimate way is to create your own image and get others to re-pin it, or pass it on. Like all social media sites, the developers are constantly updating and changing functionality so I won't discuss image sizes because they will probably change. I think it is safe, however, to say that long images (portrait) work better than wide images (landscape) because the board shape suits them better, so stick to long and slim where possible.

Make sure you use keywords relevant to your pin in the description box to enable others searching to find your work. Note that hashtags only really work as the keyword not the actual hashtag as on Twitter (where it originated from), so don't clutter the description with them.

Adding the price of a product into the description is also a good idea as there is no other place to put it, unless you add it to the image, which would look a bit messy. After all, the image is the important hook to make you want more.

Pinning strategy

Like everything you do on social media, you need to incorporate pinning into your main marketing plan to be consistent and effective, so decide what you will pin and when. A few things to consider with your pinning content strategy:

▶ Pin consistently rather than in bursts then drought periods.

▶ Pin from different sources.

▶ Pin original content where possible.

▶ Decide on keywords that need to be incorporated into your descriptions.

▶ Use many images on your website for others to pin from.

▶ Re-pin others' original content and comment on it where possible.

Activity 2

Set up at least two boards, and start adding pins to your boards.

Pinning etiquette

Pins, re-pins, commenting and liking all carry the same etiquette as on all the other sites: just be your normal, friendly self and thank others for contributing to your pins or respond to others' comments as applicable, just as you would if someone was interacting with you in reality.

Conclusion of chapter 8

Pinning is great fun as well as a great tool for many businesses, particularly food-based ones! It's also a great place to put things to review later such as articles that you come across, and I now have boards packed with things to do or read later!

If you post great images, not just good ones, you are on the right track. Happy pinning.

CHAPTER 9
Vine and Instagram basics to create great video

Key areas we will cover in chapter 9:

✓ Vine and Instagram basics

✓ using the image and video tools

✓ ideas for your business.

Vine and Instagram provide you with another set of video tools, plus Instagram is an image-sharing tool, enabling you to create and edit great footage and images to share on your other social media sites.

Quick stats www.vine.co

Here are some interesting Vine stats:

▶ it was soft launched in the summer of 2012

▶ it has over 40 million users

▶ it was acquired by Twitter in October 2012.

Quick stats www.instagram.com

Here are some interesting Instagram stats:

▶ it was launched in 2010 for photos

▶ Instagram was bought by Facebook in 2012

▶ in 2013 video of up to 15 seconds was added

▶ there are over 150 million monthly active users.

Vine

Vine is a video sharing app that runs off your smartphone, but it has a real uniqueness to it: all video recordings are a maximum of six seconds long and they loop continuously. The really cool thing with Vine is that it's very easy to use it and be creative at the same time. There really is no point creating a regular or boring video if you only have six seconds to make a splash, so think of creative ways you can use this rolling stream.

The fact that a Vine video is so short is an appeal to many people because they know from the start that it will only be that long — they don't have to click on it and wonder if it's going to be one minute or 15 minutes long and whether they can be bothered or not. It also adds some acceptability around watching a video when perhaps you should be doing something else.

Setting up your profile

Like the other social media sites, there is a profile to complete, and you can amass followers and follow others as well as re-Vine or pass on a particularly good Vine that you see. To set up your account, you will need to go to the app store and download the Vine app. It's very simple to fill out with your basic details.

Getting people to follow you on Vine is as easy as following others and hoping they will follow you back. You can also find people that you already follow on Twitter by clicking on 'find friends' on the Vine home page from your smartphone. The explore button will also put you in touch with other Vine users sorted by genre, whether it be art, comedy, food or news, so there is plenty of scope to find like-minded people. From there, just click the follow button of those that interest you and wait to see who follows you back.

Using Vine

Vine integrates nicely with Twitter and you can easily share your Vines to Facebook or embed them into your main website or blog. It took me a while to figure out how to do this because it's not obvious. From your Vine profile page using your desktop rather than your smartphone, find the video you want to share and click on the three horizontal dots that sit underneath each video. When you click on them, choose view post page and you will be given four share options: Twitter, Facebook, email and embed. This is where you also get your embed code to put directly onto your website. If you wish to actually download the whole video for some reason, the URL for this particular video will be in your browser bar and while there is not a direct download option within Vine, there are a few Vine downloader sites if you Google them.

The phone app is where it all happens rather than the desktop version, so download the app and play around with it.

Vine works best with B2C as opposed to B2B, because of the light-hearted element of the app and the creativity needed to stand out, which might not be considered serious enough for the B2B arena.

You can create a short video without the need for editing for animation or claymation or even real live subjects, it's all in the power of your touch screen, so very simple. You just need to make sure your phone stays very still for the optimum effect, so maybe use a tripod if you have one.

Vine also doesn't as yet have a search functionality built in but there are several search sites for finding great Vines or following hashtags. Keep up to date by Googling Vine search and take your pick. When you land on a Vine search platform, take a look at one particular user, Jerome Jarre. With 4.5 million followers, he has certainly found his spot on Vine and has even appeared on *The Ellen DeGeneres Show* with some of the special effect and prank Vines that he has created.

Activity 1

Have a go and create your first video. Mine was a biscuit disappearing bite by bite over six seconds. While I didn't use it in my business, it got me used to the simple way I could create something.

Using Vine in your business

By now you are probably thinking it all sounds cool, but how can my business use it?

Let's look at some examples you might try, all of which would embed nicely onto your website, share on Facebook or tweet.

Florist:

▶ putting a display together

▶ flowers opening

▶ flowers dying

▶ flowers drying

▶ delivering a bouquet

▶ making someone smile.

Garage:

▶ cleaning a car

▶ changing the oil

▶ changing a tyre

▶ happy customers

▶ repairing a dent

▶ mending a broken windshield.

Café:

▶ creating the perfect latte

▶ coffee art

▶ milk moustaches

▶ customers having fun.

Get your family to have a crack at creating something for you first off, it might just be the perfect creative video you need.

Activity 2

Make a list of the ways you could use Vine for your business using the examples in this chapter.

Vine will go from strength to strength. It's still very much in its infancy and probably appeals to the younger market through surfing the app, but if you as a brand create a great video for your website that just keeps on rolling over, how captivating would that be for your visitors? Furthermore, how many other companies in your industry have one?

Instagram

Instagram is the best image sharing app on your mobile that allows you to add creative filters to both photos and video. For example, when you have taken a photo, you can then choose one of the filter ideas to turn the image into a black and white, or sepia, or old fashioned, or brighter etc., whatever takes your fancy. These images can then be shared with your friends via both Facebook and Twitter. You can also post via email so you can either send a copy to someone, or post it to yourself for filing elsewhere.

You can, however, only share your own photos and videos. There is no option to repost them as you can on Vine, and so others cannot repost yours either. From a marketing point of view this is a bit annoying, but it's a free service you are using so you play by their rules. Maybe in the future this will change.

People can comment on your posts, though, and you can also add in a link to your website in the description just to encourage click-throughs to your brand. It's worth mentioning that hashtags rule on Instagram, probably even more so than on Twitter. Many people simply use the hashtags as the description and it seems to be accepted.

Many social media channels and Facebook in particular are using more and more images, so creating your own with easy filters means you can really post something far superior than a random stock image. It is much more personal and creative.

Using Instagram in your business

Some brands are now encouraging their customers to take Instagram pictures of themselves in the brand's clothes or with the brand's product in some way, usually for a competition. Take a look at www.nastygal.com's Instagram site http://instagram.com/nastygal# to see some of these. By asking the consumer to use the hashtag #nastygal, they are able to find them all (via Twitter usually) and collate them together for their own marketing purposes. Generally, part of the terms and conditions of the competition is that by using the designated hashtag, people are giving the brand permission to use the images. As most people that enter would love to see their name or their works of art in lights, it's not usually a problem and so everyone wins. Nasty Girl also uses www.olapic.com as a way to access these images.

Real example: Ben & Jerry's

Ice-cream brand Ben & Jerry's ran a similar competition to Nasty Girl by using the hashtag #captureeuphoria. Viewers were asked to post their Instagram pictures with their version of euphoria, so it may have included the ice cream brand or not; it didn't matter—they just wanted a great feel-good campaign. The winning Instagram images were then used in Ben & Jerry's printed advertising such as billboards, bus-stop posters and other marketing media in the local area of each winner, with a total of 25 winners in all. Imagine the winners' surprise when they picked up a magazine from their local store and their Instagram picture of euphoria was printed there. A really great feel-good campaign for both sides. Let your customers do the work for you and create great content for your brand as well as have some fun doing it.

Like Vine, Instagram appeals to the younger demographic but as Facebook now owns Instagram, and more and more people are using it, that could change and it will certainly get more and more powerful.

Instagram video

Instagram videos can use the same filter system as photos, making your 15-second videos look hip and quite different from something you shot with your video camera on your phone ordinarily. Another advantage of using the Instagram video app is that it does also populate your Instagram page on your desktop, so you can see them all in one handy place that is bigger than your mobile screen.

Many brands that run competitions where you enter by submitting a video ask that you use Instagram as opposed to any other camera or software because the entrant is then limited to 15 seconds, so everyone starts on a level playing field. These can simply be emailed to the competition email address for you to see and decide on a winner. There are also plenty of apps available to make it easy to download them, upload them and do all sorts of other things with them, and new apps seem to pop up every week, so see what suits your own needs.

Instanote

Instanote is an app that allows you to annotate an image on your phone and post it so you can create great memes on the go. It's a free app that also has a paid version which allows you to eliminate the Instanote advertising before you post. Again you can post to Twitter, Facebook, email or even text it.

Conclusion of chapter 9

Vine and Instagram are still relatively new tools and brands and people are still trying to figure out the best ways to use them. Personally, I think Instagram will be the user winner as it has the power of Facebook behind it, and the one billion users on Facebook can incorporate it into their online lives so easily, sharing videos and images with their friends.

CHAPTER 10
Making your website work and promoting your social media efforts

Key areas we will cover in chapter 10:

✓ getting the most out of your website

✓ basic search engine optimisation tips

✓ encouraging visitors

✓ ensuring consistency between your online and offline brands.

One of the great things that social media does is it pushes traffic back to your website, where hopefully your visitors will find a lot more information about your services or your products. Let's look at how we can optimise that.

Get the most out of your website

Most websites are built by a web developer who will write the code and a designer who will make the site look great visually, and there's some input from the business leader by way of content. But who is responsible for creating a website that takes the visitor on a journey, giving them the information they want in a clear and concise manner? As visitors make their way around your site, the wording may either contain chunks of jargon or be written in that corporate 'what are they trying to say' language that large companies in particular seem to use. It's almost like they are showing off using words and phrases that just don't seem to make sense to the average Joe.

You may be wondering what this has got to do with your social media efforts. Well, as you are going to be getting much more traffic to your website, it may need some attention. All of those new visitors to your site may simply turn their noses up and move on to your competition if they don't like what they see. What a waste!

Let's look at the home page on your website first. Does it do either of the following:

▶ grab your attention visually

▶ grab your attention with its headline?

Figure 10.1 is an example from the home page of a firm of drain unblockers.

Figure 10.1: web page for Danny's Drainage

> ## Let Danny's Unblock Your Drains
>
> Danny's Drainage: we strive to unblock your drains in the quickest possible time. Our company has been working on blocked drain solutions for the best part of 25 years, so our established teams know what they are doing. For all your drain solutions, look no further than Danny's.

Now compare that with figure 10.2:

Figure 10.2: improved web page for Danny's Drainage

> ## Your Drains Unblocked Fast!
> ### 4 Hour Response Time Guaranteed* find out more
>
> Danny's Drainage: the trusted name in unblocking drains, drain laying and drainage services.
>
> Hassle free, friendly, professional and expert advice. We've grown to be one of the largest specialist drainage and drain unblocking firms through a true commitment to customer service. Give us a call now!

Apart from the fact that figure 10.1 uses that stupid word 'solutions' a couple of times, it has no energy, and it certainly doesn't make me want to give them a call. If I've got blocked drains, I need action and I need it now! With a four-hour response time in the headline, and easy-to-understand, no-nonsense content in figure 10.2, pass me the phone and I am already dialling them. Which one would you call?

That home page message is so important as you only have a handful of seconds to impress a visitor and encourage them either to dig further into your website and have a look around, or to pick up the phone and call you. You do have your contact telephone number on your home page as well as your contact page, don't you? If not, you should have: don't hide it—make it easy to do business with you.

I suggest you get a couple of 13-year-olds to read your home page and 'about us' page and see if they can explain back to you what you do exactly. If they can't, you know it is too complicated for the average Joe to comprehend too, so keep the message very simple.

Activity 1

Review your website to make sure it has the following:

- an attention-grabbing headline

- clear and precise text

- your contact details, preferably top right

- nice clean images (looks professional).

There are a few more things to look at that you can change very easily to improve your site's results with search engines and also impress your visitors. I had a chat with a professional SEO company to make sure I had everything bang up to date for you, and the following is what Richard at Pure SEO came up with that needed to be included.

Headlines

In website jargon headlines are called H1 tags, which simply refer to the main heading. When someone is searching for 'drains unblocked', the Google robots rush out and find all of the pages that have that search term on the page, they sort them into order, and give you the results. Whether that search term is in the page content or in the headline, how many times it appears, and a bunch of other variables, will determine where your website listing will come up. As no-one really knows how the Google algorithm runs, we can only work with the bits that we do know. With our previous example, 'drains unblocked' appears in the headline, while the rest of the content uses slightly different words such as 'drainage' and 'drain laying'. When the robots find the pages with the search terms required, they sort the pages into order of importance, working from the top of the page down. As H1 tags are at the top of the page, you have a better chance of being found if you have those search terms in your headings.

Now you can't stuff all of your possible search terms into your headline — it would look funny and make no sense to the visitor, and it is the visitor who is going to pick up the phone and call you, not the robot. Yes, you need to be found in the first place, but don't turn visitors off when they arrive at your site. Search engines want to show relevant results for searchers, so remember when writing your headings, they must be written for your customer first and search engines second.

Content

I am amazed that the information about using search terms in your headlines just doesn't seem to get passed on from the website developer down to the person writing the content. Often the web developer will simply ask for the content you want added, and literally cut and paste it in. Your page might not even have a headline, or have something useless that won't help the search engines at all, such as 'welcome to our website'. Now you have a bit more information, you can make some alterations, and reap the rewards.

For the main bulk of the content, think about what search terms people would use to find you and make a list. Brainstorm with others, and also make use of some of the online tools such as the new Google AdWords keyword planner https://adwords.google. com/KeywordPlanner: sign in with your Google password and click on 'Search for new keyword and ad group ideas' to find what people are actually searching for. Try slightly different variations like adding an 's' on the end if it is applicable—you may be surprised at what the results tell you, but at least you can be sure of using the correct keyword. Then check how many times these keywords actually appear on each of your web pages. You may be surprised to find that they don't appear at all, which is very common. If you don't include them somewhere in your content, the robots will simply ignore your pages and they won't be found.

It's also really important not to try to beat the robots and Google; they are pretty smart at detecting when a site is overusing a keyword to try to optimise the search results. Yes make sure those keywords are there, but write great content for the person actually reading your website rather than the robot because that prospect could be the one paying your invoice.

Meta keywords

Don't worry too much about the jargon. These tags are named that way for the web guys, and they simply refer to a set of keywords that sit buried within the top of the pages of your website, and are invisible to the human eye. They are there for the robots to see. Google and the other search engines stopped putting too much emphasis on these tags some time ago as companies were filling this area with sought-after keywords that were totally irrelevant, but they brought the particular website page up whenever anyone searched using those keywords. For example, dieting and sex are multi-billion-dollar industries and are always in hot demand. By putting these 'hidden' keywords into your own website, if someone was searching for dieting, your web page on drainage potentially could come up. Web developers and marketers got wise to this and started stuffing all kinds of irrelevant but popular keywords in and Google put its foot down. Most web developers don't even bother to use this space anymore, but I think if the space is there, you may as well use it as it was intended; it can do no harm.

Page description tags

Page description tags sit on each page, again buried at the top of the page for the robots, but the humans can also see them when they do a search with Google and the descriptions of the website pages come up.

It's important that these are filled in as it's the description that you and I see when we decide whether to click on that particular search result or the next one. Therefore, a call to action is a good idea. The description needs to be 156 characters or less, as this is the limit that is shown in the search result, and should be relevant to the page it relates to. Every page on the website should have a unique description.

Ask yourself what makes you click on a particular link when you do a search? Search for your own business and see what your page descriptions say: do they make you want to click the link for more information?

I suggest that this sentence needs to include not only some of your relevant keywords, but a call to action too. 'Drains blocked? If you need your drains unblocking fast, call us today on xxxxxxx.' You don't even need to visit the website if you don't want: it has just given you its phone number right there in the search results. How easy is that!

With both the meta keywords and the description tags, you will need to have access into the 'back end' of your website where the coding sits: some content-management systems (like WordPress) will allow you into these areas to add them in. If not, it's back to your web person.

Uploading PDFs

So what other areas can you make use of to get your page ranking higher? Search robots can now read PDF files that you add into your pages: as these are usually content-rich, they are great to use.

Examples of documents for search robots

PDFs you add in will not only add value for your website visitors, but also be read by the robots. Some examples might be:

- industry reports

- white papers

- articles you have had published elsewhere

- more information about your products or services.

Page titles

This is the first thing that a search engine will look at to understand what your web page is about, and can be thought of as the most expensive real estate on your web page from a search engine perspective. These are what the name suggests, simply the title of each page, and they are visible to the visitor at the very top of the web page. You have space here to say what the page is about, which the robots can also read, so remember to add in just the right amount of keywords for it to read well.

A title tag should:

▶ contain the keywords that relate to that page

▶ be no more than 69 characters

▶ be relevant to the content on that page

▶ be unique for every page.

Image alt tags

These are alternative tags used on images. The primary function is so a visually impaired person, who may not be able to see the image, will still be able to understand what it is by using their audio website reader tools. It is also so that if an image fails to load properly, the alternative text that shows will again enable you to understand what the image is about. Another reason is so if someone is searching just for images, your alternative description may well come up in their search.

When you set your alt tags up for each image on your website, you need to not only add a proper description but also include your keywords again. Going back to our blocked drains, a picture on the home page of Danny and his truck might have the alt tag 'Danny's Drainage unblocking drains'. You get the picture?

Activity 2

Make sure you have added the following to your website:

- headlines or H1 tags
- keywords in your content
- meta keywords
- page description tags
- page titles
- alt tags.

Link building

Link building refers to how many links are pointing in to your site from other sites, and is an important part of optimising your site. If you have lots of links pointing to your site from others, that sends the robots a message that your page must be important, otherwise why would others link to you? The issue here is that not all links are equal as the authority of the page that is linking to you has a lot to do with it.

As all web pages have a page rank issued by the search engines, you really want pages linking to your site that have a page rank equal to or higher than yours. Most new or small sites rank between zero and three, with the main news sites such as CNN being way up there with eight or higher. The average for a well-maintained midrange site would be about five; I have never come across a site with the full 10 yet. If you have many links to your site from sites that have a page ranking lower than yours, it may drag your page rank down a little, so look for ways to get links from sites that are at least equal to yours or, better still, higher. Can you get an article published on your national newspaper's website or a TV station's site with a link back to yours?

To find out your own and other websites' page rank, you will need to download the toolbar from www.toolbar.google.com/T5/intl/en/features.html. When you have downloaded the toolbar, simply click on the 'wrench' icon over to the right of your screen, and in the 'tools' tab, select 'page rank'. The small green icon will then be visible on your toolbar. With each website you visit, you will be able to instantly see the page rank simply by glancing at the green icon.

A word of warning about companies that offer link exchanges through spam emails. They may sound like a good deal at the time as they link to you and you link to them, but in reality what happens is you link to them and they return the link, but in a couple of weeks' time they unlink from you, which just leaves your link to them in place. Not very fair but common practice, so the only one to win that game is the initiator of the link swap. In practice exchanging links has little to no value, the only reason to do it would be if the other website is very relevant to your business. For example, Danny's Drainage may have a link from and a link to a website that is an industry body.

One of the best ways of getting good-quality links pointing to your page is to create something called 'link bait'; this is where you have something on your website that organically makes people want to link to you. Examples of link bait could be:

▶ a free e-book

▶ an infographic

▶ a high-quality industry blog.

Webmaster tools

Go to www.google.com/webmasters/tools/&lrm and take a look around, because here you will find a whole bunch of website back-end information that you don't get in your analytics such as security and author statistics. It's free so you may as well use the information provided.

Extra URLs

Most companies have just one website with one website address, but have you thought about using several web addresses and pointing them all to the one website? If you are wondering why on earth you would want to do that, here's why:

▶ You may have a long company name.

▶ You may have a hard-to-pronounce company name.

▶ You may have a hard-to-spell or -hear company name.

▶ You wish to add keywords to your URL address.

▶ You don't want anyone else to buy that name.

Natural or clean URLs

When creating new pages throughout your website, give some thought to how the URL of the page will look, and by that I mean is it simple enough? When you are directing someone to a particular page from maybe a TV commercial or newspaper advertisement, you want to give them something that is easily remembered and easily heard. For example, Telecom's Tech in a Sec series on the TV always points back to their web page www.telecom.co.nz/techinasec rather than www.telecom.co.nz/124567techpage or something else equally hard to remember.

Keep the URL simple and containing keywords where possible and at the same time logical. The speaking page on my site is called social-media-speaker, which is exactly what the page is all about, and the page name is easily remembered and easy to pass on.

Grow your site

Each and every time you add new content to your website, the robots take note. Think of the robots as mice and your website content as their food, and boy do they like to eat. Each time you develop a new page on your site, they run off, devour it and head back home. Once they have done this a couple of times in a month they begin to see that you are providing for them on a regular basis and they make a mental note to call back to your site more frequently than to other sites that have not provided for them in a while. Keeping your website pages very active will stand you in good stead with Google and the search rankings, as this is one area that they monitor. Sites that just don't get this attention, and there are many, are further limiting their chances of being found. If you look at the main news sites, new and fresh content is being added at least daily, and so that site is growing massively over the course of a year.

Most websites are built within some sort of template, which means adding a new page is simply a matter of clicking a button or two and hey presto, you just need to add the keyword-rich, interesting content for your readers.

Having a link or widget showing your latest social media posts is a great idea as it should be regularly changing when you make new posts!

Google AdWords

This is a great way to get visitors to your site, but I am not going to go into that in this book as it is a bit of a minefield and so I suggest you get a professional to set it up for you. You can, however, set it up yourself if you are prepared to put a bit of effort into monitoring and tweaking your ads when needed. Set yourself a monthly budget that you can afford and give it a go. I would recommend getting in touch with someone who really knows it inside out and take their advice. It is very similar to Facebook ads, but without the drill-down options of who you would like to see your ad, and you may find that your competition clicks your ad just for fun as it will hit you in your pocket.

Claim your Google Places for Business page

Ever wondered how sometimes when you search there is a map that shows up and a bunch of listings, all with the little red Google location pin on them, usually from A to Z? That is where Google Places for Business comes in.

Go to www.google.com/business/placesforbusiness and set yours up. For it to work properly, you need to make sure it is fully filled out and kept up to date.

When it comes to adding your address, if you work from your home office, you may want to use your accountant's address or even a PO box address. When you have filled it all out, work on getting some reviews on your page from your clients. Aim for around six because again Google is surely going to look after those with good customer reviews when it comes to search.

Promote your social media efforts

This chapter so far has given you an overview of the areas you should be maximising on your website to get visitors. Now we'll look at how to get that all-important exposure for your social media sites, so that other people know you exist and can communicate with you.

Email signature

If you are using the professional version of Outlook you can add the icon images of your chosen sites to your email signature and hyperlink them to the relevant pages, so you can have one linking to your Facebook page, one to your Twitter page, one to your LinkedIn profile page and so on. If you don't want to use the icon images, you can simply hyperlink a short piece of text such as 'write on our Facebook wall' and it will do the same job, but you are also including a call to action at the same time.

Your emails go to people all over, not just to people in your place of work, so this is a really easy way to get some exposure for your sites, particularly when you are sending an email to a prospect as it gives that recipient a chance to see a whole lot more about your company. Your friends and family that you email will also get the benefit of keeping up with your business side if they so wish, even down to the real estate agent you have recently emailed about a possible move or the travel agent about a holiday you have just confirmed.

For those who use an email program such as Gmail, there is an option for you too called Wisestamp.com. It enables you to build your email signature and then include links to sites such as LinkedIn, Twitter and many more. You can even add random quotes that change on every email or your username for Skype, and filter in your latest tweets.

Business cards

Many companies still include their fax number on their cards and I guess that in some industries a fax machine may still be used, but if you think about yours, how often does it ring with anything that's not spam?

Use this valuable space to promote your page addresses and usernames for Skype and Twitter so that others can choose which way to communicate with you and also find further information about your company easily. Use both sides of your card so that it doesn't look too cramped. If you have to use a corporate business card that does not have all of this information on it, think about getting a second card printed with your alternative details that you can pass out alongside your corporate one.

As an aside, while we are talking about what your business card could have on it, does it have what you actually do on it too? I don't mean 'director' or other title, but if a 14-year-old picked up your card, would they understand what it is you do when they read it?

My card says 'Linda Coles, Author, Speaker and Trainer. Building relationships online', so anyone who picks up my card can see instantly what I do. What does yours say?

Printed media

People can contact you in so many different ways so wherever you would put your telephone number, think about putting your social media page details. Print media is certainly no different so think about these ideas and see if any could apply to you:

- ▶ menus
- ▶ appointment cards
- ▶ flyers
- ▶ posters
- ▶ postcards
- ▶ greeting cards
- ▶ folders
- ▶ calendars
- ▶ stickers
- ▶ vouchers

- ▶ bookmarks
- ▶ corporate gift ideas.

Don't forget to add your social site details to any adverts you run in the press and telephone directories. In fact, just think about all of the areas you publish your telephone number or web address and add them in.

Activity 3

Where will you promote your efforts? Make a list of the areas you can utilise.

Vehicle signage

Hold on, I don't mean you have to go and get your whole car sign-written at huge expense, but why not do at least the back window of your car or service vehicles? I paid a few dollars for my web address to be put in my back window and I know people have seen it because they have commented on it.

I was at a set of traffic lights in town recently when I looked across to the car at the side. I thought the driver looked familiar to me but the lights changed and off I went. When I got back to the office, there was a LinkedIn message for me from the person in that car! He had seen my back window, realised it was me and was simply saying hello. I have never actually met that person yet, only chatted on LinkedIn, but maybe one day ... I have also had people toot their horn and wave to me and I've absolutely no idea who they are but they may have chatted to me online somewhere (either that, or they are nutters).

TV and radio

If you are lucky enough to be able to afford TV or radio advertising, the same applies here. Many magazine and current affairs TV shows advertise their Facebook name at the end of each episode, inviting you over to the page after the program to leave your views and comments about the show's topics.

For big brands that are running promotions and giveaways on TV, it's the ideal place to send your traffic. You no longer need to spend large amounts of money on separate websites and applications for big promotions, just make use of Facebook.

Using your Facebook page address rather than your website means you only need a short and easy-to-remember URL. This is because the web address of any Facebook page will always be www.facebook.com followed by a forward slash and the page name, reading www.facebook.com/yourpagename. That means you only need to then tell people to go to your Facebook page 'yourpagename' and that's all they have to remember. Bear this in mind when you set your URL in the beginning, as once you have named your page it is virtually impossible to change it.

Website

Your website is also an obvious place to post links back to your social sites as your web address is usually posted on all of your printed media. Many websites simply place the icon images for Facebook, Twitter etc. on their front page somewhere at the bottom, and hope that will suffice, but it could be done better.

If your web designer is able to incorporate the icon images into the site's template so they appear automatically on every page, that would be ideal, but if not, consider adding the images to the home page, 'about' page and contact page at the very least.

Like box plug-in

The like box plug-in allows your website visitors to read the last content you loaded onto your Facebook page and become a fan of your page without ever leaving your website or viewing your page on Facebook. Your visitors can also see who else is a fan and if any of their friends are. To find the plug-in and get the HTML code to install in your website, go to Facebook and click on 'marketing' from the edit page. There you will find instructions on how to create the plug-in you require. The code will need to be installed by your web person if you can't get into the coding area yourself. You may want to add it to your blog site also if you have one.

Page backgrounds

Your Twitter page and your YouTube page will allow you to create and install an image for the whole of the background, so this is another place to add your other social site details. I use a copy of the same image from my Facebook page for continuity and because it already has my logo, my picture and my contact details, so it really is a no-brainer.

Voicemail

This may seem a crazy idea but why not? 'I'm sorry I'm not able to take your call at the moment, but why not visit my Facebook page in the meantime ...' Think of the exposure.

Blog

Recently I landed on someone's blog rather than their website looking for their email address to get in touch with them, and it simply wasn't there. Make sure your blog has your contact details, as well as links to your other social media sites. Everything should link up to everything, so check you have got all your links set up for each site. Are all of your links and your email address on your Facebook page 'info' tab too?

Newsletter

If you are regularly sending out a newsletter to your database, I hope you have your social media links on there too. I use a call-to-action text link on my newsletter rather than the image icons as it is an HTML newsletter, and I also think that you can add the relevant links into the content text seamlessly. For example, you may say, 'We have had some very interesting comments on our Facebook wall about the new chocolate-flavoured spread ...', so hyperlink the 'Facebook wall' text to go through directly to your page for them to read more. 'Write your wish list on our Facebook wall' is a good call to action and very easy for your readers to do and have a bit of fun with.

Facebook ads

We talked about Facebook ads in chapter 2. They are a very real way of publicising your pages quickly to get some traction and engagement, so decide on a budget and give them a go. Just make sure you have your content in order and your pages looking as good as they possibly can so you get the best bang for your buck.

Activity 4

Make sure you have your social media addresses or links in these areas:

- email signature
- business cards
- website
- blog
- Facebook page
- Twitter page
- LinkedIn page
- other social sites
- all print material
- newsletter text.

Is your online message the same as your offline message?

You may recall earlier in the book I mentioned a company director whose prospect had contacted him after doing his due diligence and found some discrepancies between the company's offline and online messages—it was not practising what it preached. Is your message consistent across all your forms of marketing?

Double-check the following:

▶ Is your strap line or brand promise on all of your printed and online marketing?

▶ Is your brand consistent on all of your email signatures?

▶ Do your LinkedIn profiles follow your corporate look but with some personal individuality?

▶ Are you proud of all of your tweets or do they need reining in?

▶ Does your website mirror everything in your marketing arsenal?

And if your message is consistent, is your style sheet consistent across your brand? By that I mean do you have a few branding rules in place so that visually you look consistent wherever someone may be looking at you? For example, what is the colour code of your logo, and does it match your business cards?

Rules simply give us a framework to work inside of so that the edges don't get blurred on what is acceptable and what isn't, so it makes sense to set up a style sheet to keep it easy.

Use fonts consistently

What font do you use when you are typing a quotation or letter and is it the same font as you use in your email? Does it also match the font on your website, and what about your brochures and business cards? If you use Arial 11 in all of your articles, but Calibri 12 on your website, that is not consistent and one of them may need to change.

Think about what font and what size you should have for the following on your online sites:

▶ headlines

▶ subheadings

▶ paragraphs.

I have included a checklist to help you make sure everything is covered.

Checklist

Design checklist for continuity:

- website font
- website headlines
- website subheadings
- website paragraphs
- email signature colour
- email signature text and logo
- Twitter page background
- Facebook page images
- YouTube channel background
- your other social sites
- email newsletter font
- email newsletter images
- blog font
- blog images
- all sites linked to each other where possible.

Your avatar or picture

The picture that you put out there representing your brand should be a real person where possible. Naturally, this will be impossible if you have a team tweeting behind the company brand, but for the small-business owner, the human touch is ideal. Even though it is just one computer talking to another computer, there is a real person sitting behind the screen interacting with you, and so it helps to know who you are talking to. As you change your appearance, don't be afraid to change your avatar as you go so your picture is not out of date. By keeping your picture up to date, people won't notice a big difference between your picture and you in real life.

Quick tip

Even if you can't get into the coding side of your website, do the work anyway, but make sure you get your web guy to load it up: it is important.

Conclusion of chapter 10

Your website says a lot about your brand so do make sure people can understand it and navigate it easily and that the robots can find it when someone is searching for whatever it is you have to offer. By following the easy steps in this chapter, you will be giving your website a fighting chance to generate results for you.

Wrap

I hope I have given you some ideas on how your business can make use of these online sites to seek and engage new prospects, and to add value for your current clients so that they stick around with you a good while longer. But it's all very well reading a book, you now have to put into practice what you have learned. Execute that plan!

Remember, you can always contact me through the website if you have any burning questions you need some help with. I will be only too happy to help.

Until the next book, I raise my cup of tea to your online success!

Linda Coles

Appendix A: Daisy's social media plan

Daisy's is a local flower shop with a great reputation and a loyal customer base. The team is thinking of expanding by opening another store in a neighboring town. They would also like their online sales to increase nationally.

The team starts by putting together a SWOT analysis to identify their strengths and weaknesses, and find out where the opportunities and threats will come from (see table A1, overleaf). After completing this they put together their social media plan (see table A2, overleaf), where they brainstorm about the purpose, projected achievements and outcome of the social media campaign, and identify their short- and long-term social media objectives. Finally they complete the content plan (see table A3 on p. 198), which gives them an idea of what their social media campaign will be focusing on. In this case, they will be using Facebook to create dialogue with their customers (mainly women aged 35 to 50) in the hope that they become cheerleaders for the brand.

Table A1: Daisy's SWOT analysis

Strengths	Weaknesses
• strong brand name in the local area • good online presence locally • great knowledgeable team • drive and enthusiasm • creativity • great delivery team with local knowledge	• only one location • not well known outside our location
Opportunities	**Threats**
• broaden our brand to a larger geographical area • be seen as the experts in our field • open more stores • educate our customers to get the most from their purchase • generate repeat business • focus on 'treat yourself everyday' displays for more repeat business	• other online and local florists • team could be poached by the competition • diminishing margin with cheaper competitors

Table A2: Daisy's social media plan

What is the purpose? • educate our customers on flowers and grow our brand name online • create a dialogue to engage with our customers	**What are our 12-month social media objectives?** • 1000 likes and 1000 followers and continued customer feedback • understand what our customers want and value • be the number one choice for flowers online in the local area • page 1 of Google for local flowers
What will it achieve? • customers will get more from their bouquets • relationship building with us	**What are our six-month social media objectives?** • create 500 likes and 500 followers • understand our customers' desires
What is the outcome? • be seen as the expert in the flower field • understand our customers more	**What are our three-month social media objectives?** • create 200 likes, 200 followers, customer feedback on our wall • create dialogue with our customers to find out their desires
Our target market is: Female, 35–50, loves a little luxury	**Measured by?** Google Analytics, Twitter followers, Facebook likes, increased sales/enquiries, customer feedback.
	Team: Annie and Stella primarily. All team members are free to submit articles and stories for inclusion, but Stella is accountable.

Table A3: Daisy's content plan

What is their BIGGEST problem, need or desire?	Themes for the quarter
• need flowers in a hurry • a bouquet that shows their feelings • they have forgotten an event and need to make it up to that person • a great-looking bouquet • delivery when they need it	• Valentine's Day • Easter • love • continued: flower care • quick care tips
Articles to write	**Useful videos**
• looking after your bouquet • origins of Valentine's Day • which flowers are in season during January, February and March • this year's fashionable colours • quick tips on creating your own small bouquet • what the flowers you choose mean • which flowers to buy the man in your life	Search YouTube for: • Valentine's Day funny videos • caring for your flowers Create a one-minute video on what we will be doing this Valentine's Day. Create a one-minute video on alternative gifts for Easter this year
Off-message questions	**Useful websites**
• What is the funniest Valentine's Day gift you have ever received? • Have you ever sent flowers too late? • Do you send Easter eggs to your loved ones? • How will you be celebrating Valentine's Day? • How will you be celebrating Easter this weekend?	• www.interflora.com.au • www.theflowercompany.com.au • www.valentines.com

Appendix B: Glossary

@replies Twitter term for using the @ symbol in front of a Twitter username to reply to or refer to someone, or to direct a tweet to them.

applications (apps) software to help users perform a specialised task.

bitly a service for shrinking down long URLs or web addresses.

blog a website created to share thoughts and opinions for others to see and comment on. Originally called a weblog.

boards a place to pin images on Pinterest.

business network your business connections.

business page Facebook page that can be used by a business to promote their brand and product.

cheerleaders people who love your product or service and tell their friends and networks.

community page Facebook page that can be automatically generated but can't be edited or updated.

content plan a document that describes where your online content will come from and may incorporate themes, useful websites and other resources.

Facebook   a global site that connects people socially.

Facebook ads   adverts shown only on the Facebook network.

Facebook Insights   provides analytics of your Facebook page.

forums   an online space where like-minded people chat. Can be public or private.

Google+   a social site for sharing, similar to Facebook.

Google AdWords   allows you to create adverts that are shown online in searches and on web pages.

Google Alerts   allows you to set up an alert to notify you when Google finds a post about the keyword you wish to monitor.

Google Analytics   a free service provided by Google to measure your website traffic.

Google authorship   the ability to marry up your online posts with you the author.

group page   Facebook page with different levels of security that can be used by a group of people at the same time.

Hangout   live video chat on Google+.

hashtag   term for using the hash symbol (#) to organise your information, or follow a conversation on a particular topic. It works on most social sharing sites.

HTML code   the characters and symbols used in website development.

hyperlink   a way to link a piece of online text to a web page.

Instagram   image and video sharing app.

intranet   a private online network for communicating. Usually used within larger organisations.

keywords   specific words people use to search for information online.

LinkedIn   a global business-to-business networking site.

listening post   a way of using social media to listen to what is being said about your brand or your competitors.

marketing toolkit   tools you use to market your business or brand, such as newsletters, websites, news media, TV and radio, blogs, social networking sites.

microblog   a short internet posting that gives an immediate update to followers.

networking   creating links with people to exchange ideas and information.

page description tags   help users find your website when searching through Google and other search engines for particular topics.

personal page   Facebook page that allows individuals to keep in touch with their friends on a social level.

Pinterest   online scrapbooking website and app.

pins   images posted on Pinterest.

podcast   a series of digital files in audio, similar to video but audio only.

retweet (RT)   Twitter term for sharing someone else's tweet with your followers.

recommendations   LinkedIn function where your connections can recommend you or your services to others.

return on investment (ROI)   measuring your efforts to ensure that what you are doing is returning some reward.

search engine optimisation (SEO)   search engine optimisation, or the art of your website being found on Google.

Skype   online communication tool that works in a similar way to the telephone, but through a computer or online device.

Slideshare a place to upload and share PowerPoint presentations and documents.

smartphone a mobile telephone that can also send and receive emails and can access other social applications.

social media a variety of platforms that enable users to have conversations and interact through online networks.

social media plan a document that maps out and plans your social media efforts over a fixed period of time.

social media team the people in your company who set up and manage your social media sites.

spam filter a program that prevents unsolicited or unwanted material from reaching your mailbox or website.

SWOT analysis a simple way to work out the strengths, weaknesses, opportunities and threats of your business.

target market the characteristics of your customers and those you hope to do business with.

Tweetdeck a downloadable dashboard application to make Twitter easier to use.

Twitter a social networking and microblogging service.

YouTube a global video sharing site owned by Google.

Vine a six-second revolving video-sharing app.

webinars virtual training or presentations presented through the internet.

Index

Learn more with practical advice from our experts

Start with Hello
Linda Coles

Learn Small Business Start-Up in 7 Days
Heather Smith

Web Marketing that Works
Adam Franklin and Toby Jenkins

The Social Executive
Dionne Kasian-Lew

Microdomination
Trevor Young

The Ultimate Book of Influence
Chris Helder

How to Present
Michelle Bowden

It Starts with Passion
Keith Abraham

Flee 9-5, Get 6-7 Figures and Do What You Love
Ben Angel

Available in print and e-book formats

 WILEY